On Creative Writing

NEW WRITING VIEWPOINTS
Series Editor: Graeme Harper, *University of Wales, Bangor, Wales, Great Britain*

The overall aim of this series is to publish books which will ultimately inform teaching and research, but whose primary focus is on the analysis of Creative Writing practice and theory. There will also be books which deal directly with aspects of Creative Writing knowledge, with issues of genre, form and style, with the nature and experience of creativity, and with the learning of Creative Writing. They will all have in common a concern with excellence in application and in understanding, with Creative Writing practitioners and their work, and with informed analysis of Creative Writing as process as well as completed artefact.

Full details of all the books in this series and of all our other publications can be found on http://www.multilingual-matters.com, or by writing to Multilingual Matters, St Nicholas House, 31–34 High Street, Bristol BS1 2AW, UK.

NEW WRITING VIEWPOINTS
Series Editor: Graeme Harper, *University of Wales, Bangor, Wales*

On Creative Writing

Graeme Harper

MULTILINGUAL MATTERS
Bristol • Buffalo • Toronto

To Zippy

Library of Congress Cataloging in Publication Data
A catalog record for this book is available from the Library of Congress.
Harper, Graeme.
On Creative Writing/Graeme Harper.
New Writing Viewpoints
Includes bibliographical references and index.
1. Creative writing. 2. Authorship. 3. English language–Rhetoric.
4. English language–Composition and exercises. I. Title.
PE1408.H3443 2010
808'.042-dc22 2010005054

British Library Cataloguing in Publication Data
A catalogue entry for this book is available from the British Library.

ISBN-13: 978-1-84769-257-3 (hbk)
ISBN-13: 978-1-84769-256-6 (pbk)

Multilingual Matters
UK: St Nicholas House, 31–34 High Street, Bristol BS1 2AW, UK.
USA: UTP, 2250 Military Road, Tonawanda, NY 14150, USA.
Canada: UTP, 5201 Dufferin Street, North York, Ontario M3H 5T8, Canada.

The policy of Multilingual Matters/Channel View Publications is to use papers that are natural, renewable and recyclable products, made from wood grown in sustainable forests. In the manufacturing process of our books, and to further support our policy, preference is given to printers that have FSC and PEFC Chain of Custody certification. The FSC and/or PEFC logos will appear on those books where full certification has been granted to the printer concerned.

Typeset by The Charlesworth Group
Printed and bound in Great Britain by Short Run Press Ltd.

Contents

Acknowledgements

Warm thanks must go to all those around the world with whom I have discussed Creative Writing. I owe an immeasurable debt of gratitude to each and every one of you. Without you this book would not exist. The long list of fine folk includes many fellow creative writers, of all kinds: novelists, poets, short story writers, the writers of screenplays, play scripts, writers of computer games and writers of works for children, to name just a few. Creative writers, all! To Kate Grenville, Les Murray, Jean Bedford and Tom Keneally, who in different ways ensured being a creative writer became my life. To Rob Pope. To the other wonderful folk on the Peer Review Board of the journal *New Writing*, each in their own right creatively and critically contributing to how we engage in, and understand, Creative Writing: Lisa Appignanesi, Homi K. Bhabha, Donna Lee Brien, Liam Browne (writer and Literature Director of the Dublin and Brighton Festivals), Kate Coles, Jon Cook, Peter Ho Davies, Chad Davidson, Greg Fraser, Richard Kerridge, Jeri Kroll (Onward, Jeri!), Alma Lee, Nigel McLoughlin, Andrew Motion (thanks for the gumption and the grace, Andrew), Stephen Muecke, Paul Muldoon, Nessa O'Mahony, Robert Pinsky, Harriet Tarlo, Stephanie Vanderslice Michelene Wandor, Joe Woods. To *New Writing*'s many international guest reviewers, to whom the journal owes a great deal of its continued success. To Maxim D. Shrayer of Boston College. And to Professor Drew Faust, President of Harvard University, whose presidential tenure has encapsulated the creation of the *Report of the Task Force on the Arts*, a visionary example of a university embracing the creative arts. Simply wonderful! To my students, sincere thanks. To the members of the inaugural Higher Education Committee of the UK's National Association of Writers in Education (NAWE) whose commitment to Creative Writing in universities and colleges has been unflinching. To colleagues at the Association of Writers and Writing Programs (AWP), with whom many discussions have been shared, and those of the Australian Association of Writing Programs (AAWP), likewise. Thank you. To the Peer Panellists and Practice-Led Committee Members at the UK's Arts and Humanities Research Council (AHRC) with whom I've had many lively conversations. To my fiction publisher, Parlor Press, and the wondrous editor, Dave

Blakesley, who saw an idea and boldly pursued it. The stuff of legend! To my fine, friendly colleagues of the National Institute for Excellence in the Creative Industries (NIECI) and School of Creative Studies and Media at Bangor University. And a very warm thanks to the team at Multilingual Matters; in particular, to Anna Roderick and Tommi Grover, who have been the most wonderful, engaged, informed publishers with whom to work on this book. Thank you, sincerely. And finally, and with much love, to Louise, Myles and Tyler, who keep the rhyme in the reason and help me celebrate the fiction in fact alongside the wonderful and ever present facts of fiction.

Introduction

I think that where my own confusion lies, in trying to think of 'creative' as an adjective, as some descriptive term, is in the fact that I cannot conceive of 'creative' as something available to an attitude of discreet choice, as though one were able to agree or not, as its interest quickened or wanted in one's thought of it.

Robert Creeley[1]

We can discover the origins of spoken language in the need and, perhaps also, the desire for communication by human beings with other human beings. The origins of writing systems relate to the desire and, perhaps also, the need for a system of preservation and record, that continues beyond the initial verbal utterance. But then, we might ask, why and from what human origin, comes Creative Writing?

What form of communication or, indeed, preservation and record does Creative Writing offer? What, indeed, is this set of actions, and its results, that we as human beings came to undertake it and, as continues to be the case, to encourage, and quite often admire it?[2] Why does this Creative Writing persist, so strongly, across so many cultures, undertaken by some many people, appearing in so many types, roles and locations?

It is one thing to speculate on communication and another to speculate on art. Creative Writing offers an instance of both, almost exclusively built of the most common of human communicative tools – words – adopting and adapting these to a purpose that seems at once universal and selective, simultaneously. To consider the origins of this, what must surely be our most pervasive art – on whose undertaking so many other arts rely – and our most commonly undertaken form of creative communication, would seem a natural action; yet relatively few have speculated on it, and, indeed, most of these have considered Creative Writing entirely in relation to its products, not to its *actions*. Where it has been considered in terms of its actions, not its end results, the analysis has located itself in a notion of difference or strangeness – but not in the idea of Creative Writing actions as part of our wider human landscape, where we might engage with it not as strange or because we are different but, indeed, because we are human.

What, then, is Creative Writing? Let me put forward two propositions to situate this question – though not simply to situate it in terms of its material manifestations (i.e. the physical evidence that it leaves behind) but also the metaphysical (i.e. the memories, perceptions, ideals, responses, by which we understand it). And then pose some statements as questions, to consider how (and if) these propositions offer useful insights.

Proposition I: Concerning the Nature of Creative Writing

'Creative Writing involves a set of activities, or process that can be discovered by the investigation of disseminated works.' This proposition can be considered by reference to:

(1)   Creative Writing primarily involves finished works?
(2)   Acts and actions of Creative Writing can be observed in finished works? (The definition of 'action' used here is 'a collection of acts, sometimes joined by logic, intuition or fortuitous circumstance' and the definition of act is 'something done'.)
(3)   No unfinished works are created by creative writers?
(4)   All works of Creative Writing are disseminated?
(5)   All dissemination of Creative Writing occurs, and has occurred, similarly?
(6)   There is always a direct relationship between acts and actions of Creative Writing and disseminated works?
(7)   The activities constituted as Creative Writing can always be grouped under the term 'process'?

Proposition II: Concerning Human Engagement with Creative Writing

'Creative Writing involves personal and social activities with the intention of producing art and communication.' This proposition can be considered by reference to:

(1)   All works of Creative Writing have aesthetic appeal?
(2)   All works of Creative Writing clearly communicate?
(3)   Intentions in Creative Writing are always met?
(4)   Creative Writing is solely an act or range of acts?
(5)   Personal and social activities relating to Creative Writing are always connected?
(6)   The personal and social activities of Creative Writing have equal status?
(7)   Communication and art always hold equal status in society?

One thing informs these propositional questions: that is, the human-centred nature of Creative Writing. Not merely that it is because of human action that Creative Writing exists, but that it is in human understanding that Creative Writing has evolved and continues to evolve as both an art and communication. With this in mind, statements made by creative writers reveal much, if both the actions and results of Creative Writing are kept *equally* in mind.

> [...] the freshness of flowers being arranged by the under-gardener in the cool drawing room of our country house, as I was running downstairs with my butterfly net on a summer day half a century ago: that kind of thing is absolutely permanent, immortal, it can never change no matter how many times I farm it out to my characters, it is always there with me; there's the red sand, the white garden bench, the black fir trees, everything, a permanent possession. I think it is all a matter of love: the more you love a memory, the strong and stranger it is.[3]

Vladimir Nabokov's words, spoken here in a 1962 interview with Peter Duval-Smith and Christopher Burstall. Here there is memory, there is writerly technique, there is action and thought and the presence of a representation of a certain personal materiality. But then, the word 'love'. In fact, not only the appearance of the word 'love', but the declaration that 'it is all a matter' of exactly that. Love and the exaltation, use, transference of memory to the writer's page. How, then, to incorporate love into the critical understanding of what Creative Writing might entail? Or, as is equally important, to consider the nature of love in an act, and a result, that is both art and communication? Creative writers regularly release ideals and ideas about Creative Writing. Sometimes these are incredibly individualistic, talking about their own, personal practice, their next book or poem or play, their daily lives, their loves. Other times they reference holistic entities like 'culture' or 'society', 'literature', 'readers' or 'writers'. The fact that they frequently move fluidly between the individual and holist, their personal experiences and the public ones that influence and impact upon them, is indicative of the fluidity of Creative Writing as a practice, while reminding us likewise that Creative Writing, as a range of results, rarely stays still for long.

> I was rescued by Paul Engle's Writers' Workshop in the mid-1960s, and he didn't know me, and I don't think he had ever heard of me. He didn't read that kind of crap. But somebody else out here did, and

assured him that I was indeed a writer, but dead broke with a lot of kids, and completely out of print and scared to death. So he threw me a life preserver, which is to say a teaching job. That same autumn he threw another to the world-class writer Nelson Algren, and yet another to the Chilean novelist Jose Donoso. All three of us were headed for Davy Jones's locker for sure.[4]

The ability to read or, indeed, 'hear' the differences between this piece (written by Kurt Vonnegut) and the earlier piece, by Nabokov, is distinctively human, a result of nature as well as nurture.[5] That is, we read, as we hear, in ways that relate to our individual dispositions and can be educated by circumstance, our own personal and family backgrounds, our own educations, our cultures, and our physiological conditions (e.g. what can we hear, and what do we hear in the same way as someone else?). But this piece also reveals additional, specific differences in understanding, in the way this creative writer engages with the world, in how he views his place among other creative writers, and in what he imagines words do, when placed in a certain order and situation.

How deep can we delve, then? And what dwells within here? It is not merely the individual creative writer and the individual reader. It is not merely the individual and the group or, more specifically, Vonnegut and the culture around him. It is not even simply the present (of the Creative Writing) and the past (our reading of it here, one, ten, twenty, how ever many, years after Vonnegut's death). The equality of the relationship – at least as we might imagine it – between the text in front of us, and the acts and actions of the creative writer who undertook this Creative Writing has varied, and will vary, over time and space. And the instances of engagement that this involves will draw on individual and social circumstance.

Take that word 'crap', for instance. Abrupt? Humorous? Vulgar slang? Commonplace? Colourful? Would Nabokov use it? In what way has Vonnegut used it? Of course, the sentence in which this word appears is filled with direct and indirect references to so many things. It contains a compliment to Paul Engle. It contains a reference to genre – that is, the genres that Vonnegut was working in, and around, at the time (science fiction, for example) – and it contains a comment on popular versus high culture. It also refers to the high quality of work (teaching as well as learning) being undertaken at the Iowa Writers' Workshop during Engle's time and to the nature of the experience of being a creative writer associated with that Workshop. The complexity of the experience Vonnegut is attempting to portray is no less than the concept of 'love' that

Nabokov describes, but it strikes Vonnegut differently, and this his portrayal reveals. There's also cultural and societal baggage (though 'baggage' produces perhaps too negative a connotation). Both reveal as much about their place in a cultural realm as they do about the particular creative writer's place.

To return, then, to the acts and actions, the *human* activity, that Creative Writing involves we hear (and sometimes read) all manner of clues to the nature of Creative Writing. Quite often, the mix of 'personal' and 'group' views (or, we could say, 'individualist' and 'holist' views; or, even, 'single' and 'collective' views) is complex and highly developed. It is the result of interactions of circumstance, knowledge and under-standing, throughout time. Frequently, it contains both direct and indirect references to action and thought. Always it reveals some of the ideas and ideals of the creative writer as they involve themselves in Creative Writing. Take, for example, this from Nobel Prize winner Toni Morrison, delivered to the American Writers Congress in October 1981. She is referring, initially, to a comment she's made earlier ('We are toys [...]'), in relation to commercialism and a publishing obsession with financial success:

> That this notion of the writer as toy – manipulable toy, profitable toy – jeopardizes the literature of the future is abundantly clear. But not only is the literature of the future endangered; so is the literature of the recent past. This country has had an unsurpassed literary presence in the world for several decades now. But it will be lucky, in the coming decade, if it can hold its own. What emerges as the best literature of the 1980s or even the 1990s may be written elsewhere by other people. Not because of an absence of native genius but because something is very wrong in the writer's community. Writers are less and less central to the idea and subject of literature. Whole schools of criticism have dispossessed the writer of any place whatever in the critical value of his work. Ideas, craft, vision, meaning – all of them are just so much baggage in these critical systems. The text itself is a mere point of departure for philology, philosophy, psychiatry, theology and other disciplines.[6]

Here we can hear Morrison's ambition – in the year she turned 50, seven years before she won the Pulitzer Prize for Fiction and twelve years before she won the Nobel Prize for Literature. We can hear a creative writer with pride and energy. A creative writer, also, with a critical eye on the nation around her, and a clear sense of the audience she is addressing.

We hear, also, in words such as 'jeopardizes' and 'unsurpassed' not only a creative writer with a passion for the political inference of writerly action, but a writer with a desire to address themes of structural and functional conflict. That is, the kind of conflict that arises from some systemic wrong, some unstable yet established entity, which moves as long term history or as part of an historical cycle. This is different in philosophy from the interpretation of our world as consisting of random events scattered over a societal container made up of individuals. Historical structure matters here; individuals are not tied down entirely by materialities, but they're not able to operate free of them either. In other words, speaking in shorthand, it is not difficult to imagine Morrison, the creative writer, writing a novel such as *Paradise* (1993), in which she portrays conflict between two relatively structured communities.

Of course, Creative Writing isn't as simple as that. Suffice it to say, human activity almost never can be reduced to a single plain of under-standing. So we cannot simply go through the pronouncements of creative writers and reconstruct the nature of Creative Writing from their outpourings, even those outpourings that relate to their creative practices. Similarly we cannot, simply, discover the nature of Creative Writing in the scrawls on the margins of their manuscripts or in the letters or emails they send to friends, or in the paintings, films, plays, sports, their admire, in their choice of desk, or in the instrument or technology their use to write. We cannot, simply, take biographical fact and, on the basis that the subject is a creative writer, make from these the very fact of Creative Writing. And yet, we cannot do without these either.

The artefactual evidence of the act and actions of Creative Writing – whether notes and scribbles, complementary works (those pieces of writing, creative and otherwise, that are produced alongside primary Creative Writing activity), final works or 'post-works' (those responses that follow the 'completion' and/or dissemination of Creative Writing) – this artefactual evidence adds to the things that creative writers say, verbally, some of which are quoted in writing, about what they do, why they do it, and how the relationship between the acts and actions of Creative Writing and its final, or even preliminary, results interrelate. These things are pointers, directional guides to what Creative Writing entails, what it is, as a human practice. Thus, Yevgeny Yevtushenko:

> A poet's autobiography is his poetry. Anything else can only be a footnote. A poet is only a poet when a reader can see him whole as if he held him in the hollow of his hand with all his feelings, thoughts, and actions.[7]

In general, in spite of all the intrigues and the dirt that go with it, sport is a cleaner business than literature. There are times when I am very sorry I did not become a footballer.[8]

Yevtushenko, a creative writer not without the ability to polarise opinion, offers at least some indication of how he and those who respond to his work interact. Likewise, he grounds his writerly identity in his writerly action – suggesting, even if only briefly, that the relationship between his sense of self and his sense of the cultural community in which he works or worked (because these statements were published in 1963) is the site of personal choice and public tension, personal concern and public distance. Compare that with these words from Margaret Atwood, talking about the writing of her *The Handmaid's Tale* (1985):

> How did *The Handmaid's Tale* get written? The answer could be, partly on a rented electric typewriter with a German keyboard in a walk-up flat in West Berlin, and partly in a house in Tuscaloosa, Alabama – which, it was announced to me with a certain pride, is the per capita murder capital of the United States. 'Gosh,' I said. 'Maybe I shouldn't be here.' 'Aw, don't y'all worry,' they replied. 'They only shoots family.' But although these two places provided, shall we say, a certain atmosphere, there is more to the story than that.[9]
>
> While I was writing it, and for some time after, I kept a scrapbook with clippings from newspapers referring to all sorts of material that fitted in with the premises on which the book is based – everything from articles on the high level of PCBs found in polar bears, to the biological mothers assigned to SS troops by Hitler, in addition to their legal wives, for the purposes of child production, to conditions in prisons around the world, to computer technology, to underground polygamy in the state of Utah. There is, as I have said, nothing in the book without precedent. But this material in itself would not constitute a novel. A novel is always the story of an individual, or several individuals; never the story of a generalized mass.[10]

Interesting, here, that Atwood should be drawn to talk about 'precedent'. Equally interesting that she should focus on the content research that she undertook in the writing of the book, and that she recalls so much of the physical circumstances of the writing, even down to the fine detail of the kind of typewriter used and the entries made in a scrapbook. These, previously unpublished comments were made in 1989 and eventually published in a book edited by Atwood, *Writing with Intent*, in 2005. We can confidently assume that Atwood was happy to see the comments published, because she was the editor of the book in which they appear. We cannot, perhaps, *absolutely* ascertain if she clarified, altered or in any way rewrote (however minutely) sections of this, described in her bibliography as an 'unpublished speech' – though she does suggest that she did not. In fact, we can reasonably safely conclude that Atwood recognised the changes in circumstances, in location in life, in personal Creative Writing history – all those evolutionary aspects – because she tells us she considered exactly that:

> Looking back at some of these essays – 'essays' in the sense of 'attempt' – I feel I might write them in another way if I were writing them today. But then, I'd be unlikely to write them today. Everything we do is embedded in time, and time changes not only us, but our point of view as well.[11]

Speaking crudely, then, Atwood is covered! If what appears in her book of 'essays, reviews, personal prose' is not what she currently believes or, indeed, is changed by a lapse in memory or the impact of later occurrences, then this fact can be assigned to changes in 'point of view'. Not that any of this is necessarily orchestrated by the creative writer in order to dupe the reader. Atwood, like anyone else, is situated in time; and yet, she has the ability (via memory) to transcend linear chronology. The fact that she transcends linear chronology, in part, in the act and actions of Creative Writing is our focus here.

Creative Writing occurs in motion. Creative writers experience Creative Writing this way. Cynthia Ozick, for example:

> To return to the matter of credentials. A bird can fly over any continent you choose; it's the having the wings that counts. A writer can be at home in novel, story, essay or play; it's the breathing inside a blaze of words that counts.[12]

Motion, movement, activity. Similarly, Creative Writing exists, for creative writers, as perception, memory and action first, and as object and result second. This needs emphasising. *Creative Writing, for creative writers, is first and foremost perception, memory and action* because it is in perception, memory and action that creative writers become, and remain, creative writers. And it is in action that the Creative Writing becomes defined. That is: if the creative writer cannot act in order to pursue the writing of something, then they cease to be creative writers. They may have *been* creative writers, they may even have an existence 'in memory', as creative writers; but they are no longer such. For this reason – though not solely this reason – creative writers live equally for the greater parts of their daily lives in the worlds of perception, memory and/or action. Were they to live mostly in the worlds associated with specific physical results (e.g. a 'final' draft, a work completed) and physical objects (e.g. a 'published' novel, poem, shooting script) then they would cease to function as creative writers; and certainly, at points in their careers, this cessation would prevent them from evolving as creative writers. Muriel Spark:

> I must say that my rejection slips, if they fell out of the envelopes at a rate of more than two a day, depressed me greatly. However, I had a list of possible weeklies and little magazines to hand, and immediately I put the poem or article into a new envelope with a letter to the editor and S.A.S.E. If the work I was offering looked shopworn, I would type it out again. The money for these stamps for outgoing mail was a pressing part of my budget in those days.[13]

Spark's recollections here are those of a tyro artist; and they are certainly those of the determined apprentice seeking approval for what they are achieving or, in part, what their promise suggests they might achieve. But that is not all that is being said. There is a systemic sense to the way the which Spark acts and reacts. And there's an emotional and dispositional aspect, which she reveals openly, seemingly without pretence. Behind this short story of struggle there is, also, intention and meaning (both personal and cultural meaning). There are feelings and reasons, which in themselves reveal much about Spark, but also much about the nature of Creative Writing and its place in the human world. There are behaviour patterns, intricate ones. There is personal psychology and the echo of group psychology. And there is a set of cultural and social rules and relationships that not only impact on action, but also on thought, and also on the ways in which perception is formed, or memory devolved, influenced or applied.

Consider, in this vein, Spark's very determined need to retype a manuscript that returned to her 'shopworn'. We could consider this activity merely in terms of the niceties of the publishing industry at the time or, additionally, consider the sense of pride Spark felt in the appearance of her work. But what else? What lies beneath this simple, somewhat methodical, act? Could it be something to do with a wider interest in appearance? Could it be some physiological need, relating to feelings of rejection or the desire for acceptance? Could it be a form resistance? Or could Spark employ it as an act of bold declaration? Whatever interpretation we place on just that one act (of the many described in even the short quote, above) it is clear that this is an undertaking of some importance, that (in this case) it left some physical evidence, and that it carries evidence (both physical and metaphysical) about the nature of Creative Writing.

Add to this the consideration that time – as Henri Bergson pointed out so well in his work, *Time and Free Will: An Essay on the Immediate Data of Consciousness*[14] and *Matter and* Memory,[15] among others – real time is not subject to the linearisation or compartmentalisation; rather, it is durational, fluid, unable to be measured by the methods of science or considered as a series of moments [AQ: Have changed 'series' from 'serious' OK?]. Memory plays a role in a contemporaneous way, alongside that which exists physically around us, and in conjunction with perception. In addition, not all memory has immediate impact on action, or even has perceived relevance for the actions being undertaken. So, rather than seeing Creative Writing acts and actions as determined only by the observed elements of 'now', or by perception based entirely in direct and immediate links between memory and actions, it is important to recognise that perception, memory and action interact fluidly, that this interaction is complex and multifaceted and that notions of chronology determined by the emergence of objects (e.g. works of Creative Writing) is only part of this story. It is impossible to determine what Creative Writing is, how it exists, why human beings undertake it, or even to accurately interpret the evidence that Creative Writing produces without recognition of this fact. Creative writers are negotiating this area constantly. The following questions, and their investigation, suggest ways we can approach this very human activity.

Notes

1. The Creative Robert Creeley, *MLN* 89(6), Comparative Literature, December 1974, 1029–1040, 138–139.
2. Daniel Nettle suggests that 'When a cultural invention like Creative Writing comes along, it will flourish if it is successful at capturing the attention and motivation of a significant number of people, and it will wither if it does not' (p. 102). Intriguingly, he also goes on to suggest there may be certain 'evolutionary' advantages associate with Creative Writing (p. 109). Nettle, D. (2009) The evolution of Creative Writing. In *The Psychology of Creative Writing*, Cambridge University Press, p. 101.
3. Nabokov, V. (1974) BBC Television 1962. In *Strong Opinions*. London: Weidenfeld and Nicolson.
4. Vonnegut, K. (1999) New World Symphony. In *A Community of Writers: Paul Engle and the Iowa Writer's Workshop*. Iowa City: University of Iowa Press, p. 115.

5. Not to say, of course, that this is not complex. Alberto Manguel writes: 'Whether reading is independent from, for instance, listening, whether it is a single distinctive set of psychological processes or consists of a great variety of such processes, researchers don't yet know, but many believe that its complexity may be as great as thinking itself.' Manguel drawing from Merlin C Whittrock's work on reading comprehension. Manguel, A. (1996) *A History of Reading*. London: Harper Collins, p. 39.

6. Morrison, T. (2008) For a heroic writers' movement. In Carolyn C. Denard (ed.) *What Moves at the Margin: Selected Nonfiction*. Jackson: University of Mississippi pp. 157–158.

7. Yevtushenko, Y. (1963) *A Precious Autobiography*. London: Collins & Harvill, p. 7

8. Yevtushenko, Y. (1963) *A Precious Autobiography*. London: Collins & Harvill, p. 58.

9. Atwood, M. (2005) Writing Utopia. In *Writing with Intent: Essays, Reviews, Personal Prose, 1983–2005*. New York: Carroll & Graf, p. 92.

10. Atwood, M. (2005) Writing Utopia. In *Writing with Intent: Essays, Reviews, Personal Prose, 1983–2005*. New York: Carroll & Graf, pp. 99–100.

11. Atwood, M. (2005) Writing Utopia. In *Writing with Intent: Essays, Reviews, Personal Prose, 1983–2005*. New York: Carroll & Graf, pp. xiii–xiv.

12. Ozick, C. (2003) On being a novice playwright. In Maria Arana (ed.) *The Writing Life: Writers on How they Think and Work*. New York: Public Affairs, p. 257.

13. Spark, M. (2003) Emerging from under your rejection slips. In Maria Arana (ed.) *The Writing Life: Writers on How they Think and Work*. New York: Public Affairs, p. 54.

14. Bergson, H. (1910) *Time and Free Will: An Essay on the Immediate Data of Consciousness* (F.L. Pogson, trans.). London: George Allen and Unwin.

15. Bergson, H. (1911) *Matter and Memory* (N.M. Paul and W. Scott Palmer, trans.). London: George Allen and Unwin.

PART I

CONCERNING THE NATURE OF CREATIVE WRITING

Creative Writing involves a set of activities, or process, that can be discovered by the investigation of disseminated works.

This proposition can be considered with reference to:

Chapter 1
Creative Writing Primarily Involves Finished Works?

1.

When speaking about 'Creative Writing' it is sometimes the case that we are speaking about two things. That is: the activities of Creative Writing *and* the finished works that emerge from the activities of Creative Writing. However, most often the term 'Creative Writing' is used to refer to the activities we engage in. The results of these activities, alternatively, are most often referred to by their specific 'artefactual' names – for example, the 'poem', 'script', 'story' or 'novel' that emerges from the acts and actions of Creative Writing.

This separation in language also represents a separation in attitude, a separation that was extended by the strength of the focus during the 20th century on the objects, the 'finished' artefacts, of creative production. This was particularly the case in the second half of the 20th century when consumerist ideologies, supporting an economic system increasingly dependent on the exchange of goods and services, made material goods a primary mode of human exchange, and the provision of services likewise became highly commodified. In a metropolitan rather than rural focused production system, no longer trading in a relatively leisurely fashion in hand-crafted objects or in a close community of labour exchange, consumerism involved product and purchaser, the role of the producer – at least as it pertained to the recognition of the individual, or to place of the personal – grew less significant. That is not to pass judgement on the impact of consumer culture in the latter half of the 20th century. Rather, it is simply to note that the rise of consumerism relied on the significance of goods and services for consumption and on the desire, and ability, of the consumer to purchase these goods and services. If there was a producer referenced at all the role of producer 'branding' was more notable than the *actual* activities of that producer.

Of course, the word 'production' is being used instead of the words 'Creative Writing' or 'creating', to indicate this was a consumption and production cycle of a distinct kind and that it impacted upon how we viewed Creative Writing. In the case of Creative Writing, the words 'creative writer', or 'creator' or 'maker' might seem more appropriate to indicate the often individual nature of the acts and actions of Creative Writing and to highlight the fact that not every piece of Creative Writing was destined to a commercial exchange. Indeed, this is part of a point worth developing later. Here, however, the important aspect of the historical profile is that it was *product-consumption* related, even while culturally the latter 20th century saw the rise of individualism and the declarations of the importance of individual voices. In the case of economics, it was not the individual human 'maker' who held sway but the individual human 'receiver'. This was a cycle dependent on the willingness of individuals to purchase, to receive according to trade focused on artefactual brand (even in the case of services where commodification used almost identical rhetoric or the imagery of offering 'satisfaction').

Language, then, whether verbal or visual, whether denotative or connotative, bore the significance of finality, the importance of completed 'works', and demoted the relevance of 'working' or 'undertaking' to a secondary rank in which efficiency, delivery to the market, adherence to a promoted brand, and clarity of what was on sale, far outweighed the accuracy of production information. Indeed, while later in the century evidence of some Western concern with 'fair trading' or 'exploitation' of non-Western producers became evident, for the greater part of the 20th century the West, where consumerism most strongly flourished, devoted itself far more to delivery of goods and services than it did to the question of how – physically or, indeed, ethically – these goods and services were delivered. This focus on end commodity result even bore an alternate moral standing by which the product, in the broadest sense of the term, was *expected* to be available when and where the consumer required it. The moral imperative of satisfying the consumer came in many guises, not merely in terms of quantity or quality, and certainly not only relating to the initially observable appearance of the good or service. Rather, it carried with it symbolic and cultural intention, high culture, low culture, 'well-made', 'poorly-made', 'expensive', 'cheap', significant or insignificant for one cultural group or another, whether the dominating or dominated. Categories and ideals that transgressed the boundaries of the material, but were always entirely tied to it.

We could take this historical perspective back further for Creative Writing and note that such a separation of the 'finished' artefact from the acts and actions of creative writers owed much to the commodification borne on the back of the ideal of copyright. Copyright, founded as it was on the 'concept of the unique individual who creates something original and is entitled to reap a profit from those labors'.[1] And yet already can be observed the deductive shift, because in this definition the conflating of 'something' with 'labours' locates copyright in end, indeed final, result rather than in the labour, or creating itself.

From this perspective, we can extend such analysis to show how we have seen considerable importance placed on 'works' rather than on the human 'work' of creation. So, for example, Martha Woodmansee, writing in her chapter in *The Construction of Authorship: Textual Appropriation in Law and Literature*, asks:

> Will the author in the modern sense prove to have been only a brief episode in the history of writing? By 'author' we mean an individual who is the sole creator of unique 'works' the originality of which warrants their protection under laws of intellectual property known as 'copyright' or 'authors' rights.[2]

This is a reasonable question to ponder, if we begin with 'works' rather than 'working', because if authorship is located in the ownership of completed artefacts then of course the authors of *The Construction of Authorship* are right to ask whether such a concept has any permanency. Ownership of artefacts has to be seen as fragile because artefacts can be exchanged, can be traded, can be sold, valued and re-valued, placed on the market, or stored for future exploitation. But what about actions?

What about the acts and actions that a creative writer, or group of creative writers, undertake? Once undertaken – even *while* being undertaken – who owns these? If they are not contracted to someone else – say in the case of a film script or novel produced according to a pre-writing contract – if they are not contracted to someone else, can anyone other than the creative writer or writers ever own them? Indeed, to be entirely accurate, what *actually* is it that is contracted if the writing of a work is contracted? It is not the act or actions of the creative writer that, say, the film company of publisher has contracted; rather it is the work or works they produce. They have, most definitely, contracted the labour, but if the labour produces only labour and no result, would the contract be seen to have been met? This question, too, we might visit later. But, for now, suffice to say it would be an unusual circumstance that would see a creative writer contracted simply to write but never to be expected to deliver some work or works to those who had contracted them.

The subject of Jaszi and Woodmansee's book is copyright and 'appropriation' and it would be churlish to criticise their conclusions.

They place their focus on artefacts and their contributors produce clear analyses of copyright vested in objects and products. But shift the point at which the analysis begins away from artefacts and towards the acts and actions of creative writers and Woodmansee's consideration of whether authors will continue to exist becomes erroneous. Of course, authors will continue to exist as long as we continue to undertake the acts and actions of authorship. I take authorship here to be the *activity* of authoring; and, of course, I am speaking of the practical and, indeed, physiological as well as psychological act of *creating*, not about whether interpretation of the works of others is a form of authoring, or about whether authorship is as much a wider cultural activity as well as an individual one, or about whether the word 'author' may mean something other than the 'physical' commonsense concept of the 'maker'. Naturally, this approach brings together the idea of the 'creative writer' with the idea of the 'author' and that, in itself, raises many questions. But because this conflation has also been generically, colloquially and even critically undertaken by many others, it would seem simplest to let it remain, at least for now.

Jaszi and Woodmansee are not unaware of the problems in all this, explaining in their Introduction that:

> To merit copyright an 'expression' must be 'fixed,' leading to the exclusion of a wide range of improvised works and works of oral tradition.[3]

Again, entirely accurate. And yet, how many acts or actions of creative writers are fixed and how many are in motion, part of a continuum of action, inseparable from the action beside them, before them, or after them? Naturally, a ridiculous question because human actions are only able to be separated from each other if we stop them. If we stop them they are, by simple definition, no longer acts and actions but *past* activities that might be reflected upon, even if then they are altered by their relationship with fixity, and now also altered by their relationship with any current or future acts and actions that may be undertaken. To recall some related comments by Henri Bergson briefly:

From *Creative Evolution*:

> Let us start, then, from action, and lay down that the intellect aims, first of all, at constructing. This fabrication is exercised exclusively on inert matter, in this sense, that even if it makes use of organised material it treats it as inert, without troubling about which animated it. And of insert matter, fabrication deals only with the solid; the rest escapes by its very fluidity.[4]

From *Time and Free Will*:

On the one hand we attribute to the motion the divisibility of the space which it traverses, forgetting that it is quite possible to divide an *object*, but not an *act*: and on the other hand we accustom ourselves to projecting this act itself into space, to applying it to the whole of the line which the moving body traverses, in a word to solidifying it: as if this *localizing* of progress in space did not amount to asserting that, even outside consciousness, the past coexists along with the present![5]

From the *Creative Mind*:

I was indeed very much struck to see how real time, which plays the leading part in any philosophy of evolution, eludes mathematical treatment. Its essence being to flow, not one of its parts is still there when another part comes along.[6]

And later:

I very quickly spotted the inadequacy of the associationist conception of the mind; this conception, then common to most psychologists and philosophers, was the result of an artificial re-grouping of conscious life. What would direct vision give – immediate vision, with no interposed prejudices?[7]

And this from *Time and Free Will*:

The whole difficulty of the problem that occupies us comes from the fact that we imagine perception to be a kind of photographic view of things, taken from a fixed point by that special apparatus which is called an organ of perception – a photograph which would then be developed in the brain-matter by some chemical or psychical process of elaboration. But is it not obvious that the photograph, if photograph there be, is already taken, already developed in the very heart of things and at all the points of space? No metaphysics, no physics even, can escape this conclusion. Build up the universe with atoms: each of them is subject to the action, variable in quantity and quality according to the distance, exerted on it by all materials atoms.[8]

That is probably enough of a selection from Bergson's philosophical writings to give a flavour of them to those unfamiliar with his work, and enough to suggest equally how a concentration on fixity, and a failure to deal adequately with the active aspects of human activity, human creativity, relates to recognising Creative Writing as acts and actions, and how this might thus relate to the *actual* status of 'completed' works of Creative Writing.

If, on first thought, the sense in which a work of Creative Writing is 'complete' when released to a readership or audience suggests we might use these 'completed' works as focal points for a consideration of the acts and actions that produced them, then Bergson's work certainly asks us to think again about how we co-locate such discussions with those about Creative Writing itself. Equally, the statements of creative writers about their activities frequently undermines the suggestion that completed works are ever – in the sense of what Creative Writing actually *is* – ever truly complete. To take the comments of one of Henri Bergson's near contemporaries, Ernest Hemingway:

> When you are excited about something is when the first draft is done. But no-one can see it until you have gone over it again and again until you have communicated your emotion, the sights and sounds to the reader, and by the time you have completed this the words, some-times, will not make sense to you as you read them, so many times have you re-read them. By the time the book comes out you will have started something else and it is all behind you and you do not want to hear about it. But you do, you read it in covers and you see it all the places that now you can do nothing about it.[9]

Hemingway expressing here the creative writer's desire to 'do [some-thing] about it', to take action to correct some element of their writing that notions of the object, of finality, of completeness, denies them easy access to correct. To stay in broadly the same period, add to this these observations from the diaries of Virginia Woolf:

This from Sunday 22 January 1922:

> [...] The birds wake us with their jangling about 7 o'clock; which I take to be a sign of spring, but then I am always optimistic. A thick mist, steam coloured, obscures even twigs, let alone Towers Place. Why do I trouble to be so particular with facts? I think it is my sense of the flight of time: so soon Towers Place will be no more; & twigs, & I that write. I feel time racing like a film at the Cinema. I try to stop it. I prod it with my pen. I try to pin it down.[10]

And this from Saturday 2 August 1924:

> [...] honestly I don't feel old; & it's a question of getting up my steam again in writing. If only I could get into my vein & work it thoroughly

deeply easily, instead of hacking out this miserable 200 words a day. And then, as the manuscript grows, I have the old fear of it. I shall read it and find it pale. I shall prove the truth of Murry's saying, that there's no way of going on after Jacob's Room. Yet if this book proves anything, it proves that I can only write along those lines, & shall never desert them, but explore further & further, & shall, heaven be praised, never bore myself an instant.[11]

'No way of going on.' The fear of having no way of proceeding, of continuing. To continue to be a creative writer someone must be writing, creatively. Simple as this statement appears, might it be the core of why completed works do not constitute Creative Writing? Not to emphasise here any argument for Woolf having a fragile psyche, a notion that has been too great a focus for some biographers and critics over the years. And, inadvertently, have I picked up comments by two creative writers who chose to depart the world in, dare I say it, broadly similar ways? Then perhaps best to add an alternate. This from South African playwright and novelist Athol Fugard:

August:

> After the long sweat of reshaping and rewriting, now entered a phase in my work on the third act of *People* which I can almost say I 'enjoy'. My line is sketched roughly on paper so there is no longer any of the tension involved in moving from moment to moment, and of finding those moments. But it is a rough line. Now I refine – Somewhere else in the notebooks I have spoken about this – likened it to passage of time, a mechanism which once evolved can be wound up again and again and allowed to run down.[12]

An intriguing combination of analogical thoughts here: 'evolution', the 'winding up' and 'running down', the 'finding' of 'moments', the 'rough line'. It is often the language used to describe creative practice that alerts us to the fact that there are combinations of the individual and societal or cultural at work. Depending on the writer, these emerge more or less obviously, appearing on the surface of the language of creating or suggesting by more oblique reference that they are there beneath it. But the focus remains activity, an undertaking without separations. It is not merely a sense of wanting to do better, achieve more, that is recalled here in the diaries, letters or notebooks of Woolf and Hemingway and Fugard but the sense that completeness, artefactual existence, does not equate to the Creative Writing lives in which they are personally engaged.

2.

For some centuries now, finished works of Creative Writing have been highly valued if they have met certain criteria, and matched certain expectations, whether these have been defined by the nature of writing as communication, the cultural worth of particular forms and genre at particular times in history, aesthetic evaluations also based in historical or cultural conditions, the social position of a particular creative writer, or the conditions of dissemination – for example, the rise of the market for commercially published books, the power of bookseller, the impact of the world wide web. This is no bad thing for any of us who believe Creative Writing brings something important to the world – both as an activity and as a producer of works.

However, to varying degrees, the evolution of the market for Creative Writing created a greater emphasis on the final physical results of the acts of Creative Writing and therefore increased the product value of Creative Writing. The final product value remains today the most recognised (if not, we might realise, the most important) value of Creative Writing in a capitalist, consumerist society – which is the primary economic and political environment for the vast majority of Creative Writing produced in the world.

With this in mind, finished works of Creative Writing represent Creative Writing's commodity value and such commodity value carries not only the weight of industry but also the weight of governmental or public worth because its contribution to society can be easily measured and comparative analysis can yield functional results. By functional results is meant the kinds of results that produce commercial policy (for example, that determine a publisher's investment in a new finished work of Creative Writing, or in the contracting of a work to be written) or, indeed, that determine a government's investment in public under-takings (for example, in the support of the creative and cultural industries sector, the development cultural quarters within the remits of environ-mental and town planning, and the archiving or display of cultural products, libraries, museums, educational resources).

However, the commodity value of finished works of Creative Writing is not one-dimensional. Two mechanisms of value are at play:

(1)   finished works of Creative Writing as commercial commodities;
(2)   finished works of Creative Writing as cultural commodities.

The value of finished Creative Writing as commercial creative com-modity lies in its ability to capture a paying audience. With this in mind, finished works of Creative Writing that rely on their value commercially display a range of often clearly highlighted characteristics. These are works that can be readily recognised by the general consumer/reader – for example, works that do not require specialist knowledge of what most commonly might be called 'literature'. So these works, more often than not, conform to mainstream notions of Creative Writing and consumption/reading. They may be works that, to take a well known consideration, fit easily into definitions of genre (for example, the crime novel, the script of the comedy film or of the fantasy computer game; the 'celebrity novel'). They may be works that, because of considerable commercial investment, require considerable marketing in order to meet their commercial expectations.

Finished works of Creative Writing whose value is located *primarily* in their commercial worth may or may not be well-received by critics whose focus is on analysing the quality of those finished works. That is to say, a finished work of Creative Writing that is popular with a wide readership or audience can also achieve critical acclaim. However, commercially successful works of Creative Writing that do not receive critical acclaim – or, indeed, are dismissed entirely by critics and scholars – still can have recognised value and that value, while of a different kind to that perhaps favoured by professional critics and scholars is not necessarily lesser in terms of the activities of the creative writers who undertake such work.

However, Creative Writing also can have a different, or in some cases *additional*, commodity value. That is, the commodity value created by professionalised critical acclaim itself. It cannot have escaped anyone's notice that the commodity value of certain final works of Creative Writing became higher when critical opinion became professionalised – that is, in the birth of the study of 'Literature' and in the evolution of the professional and often academically informed literary press. This too owes much to the conditions prevailing during the 20th century, not least in Higher Education as the expansion of the university and college sector initiated the expansion of the mechanisms much needed to support it. As Andrew Delbanco pointed out at the very end of the 1990s:

> Literature in English has been a respectable university subject for barely a century. The scholar of Scottish and English ballads Francis James Child was appointed to the first chair in English at Harvard in 1876; the English honors degree was not established at Oxford until 1894.[13]

So, indeed, the cultural commodification of final works of Creative Writing – so that, to put it crudely, academic critics, whose profession it has been to highlight and discuss literary cultural and cultural literary worth, become simply another kind of consumer[14] – such cultural commodification has further focused on final results of the acts and actions of creative writers, rather than on the less graspable acts and actions themselves and it has done so in support of the value of the final creative artefact, both to the detriment of discussions about creative practices and to the benefit of those creative writers who have met the requirements of such cultural commodification. Much like commercial commodification, cultural commodification has relied on instruments – copyright, in the case of the commercial; the professionalisation of education and of a subject within education in the case of cultural commodification. And something of an analogical condition to this described by Geoffrey Turnovsky in relation to the Enlightenment literary market, Rousseau and 18th-century France has prevailed:

> But to the extent that the book trade was idealized as a transparent mediating field, in its reality, it was also confronted by its author in its denseness and opacity, as a sphere controlled by agents who, despite their social neutrality, did not necessarily share, understand, or even conceive of Rousseau's literary–ethical project. The resulting contradictory image of the book trade, as the ambiguous product of both a deep desire for authorial self-expression and an inexorable doubt about the possibility of such self-representation in the depersonalized realm of commerce, was the literary market conceptualized, constructed and depicted [...][15]

And so we see a separation between acts and actions of Creative Writing and the 'finished' artefacts of Creative Writing, born on both commercial and cultural commodification, supported by instruments of ownership and education, and perpetuated by the needs of a consumer market which relied on centralised modes of exchange which did not alter greatly before the very end of the 20th century when was witnessed the birth of new technologies in the form of the world wide web (WWW) and, later, mobile telephony, which dispersed the means of dissemination and changed the dynamic of making and revealing creative practice. For now, suffice it that finished works of Creative Writing have held sway on how we perceive what Creative Writing is, but that this has not been because such an assumption is correct.

Notes

1. Rose, M. (1994) *Authors and Owners: The Invention of Copyright*. Cambridge (MA): Harvard University Press, p. 2.
2. Woodmansee, M. (1994) On the author effect: recovering collectivity. In P. Jaszi and M. Woodmansee (eds) *The Construction of Authorship: Textual Appropriation in Law and Literature*. Durham (NC): Duke University Press, p. 15.
3. Jaszi, P. and Woodmansee, M. (eds) (1994) *The Construction of Authorship: Textual Appropriation in Law and Literature*. Durham (NC): Duke University Press, p. 11.
4. Bergson, H. (1998) *Creative Evolution*. New York: Dover, first published in English in 1911, p. 153.
5. Bergson, H. (2001) *Time and Free Will*, New York: Dover, first published in English in 1913, p. 112.
6. Bergson, H. (1994) *The Creative Mind: An Introduction to Metaphysics*. New York: Citadel, p. 10.
7. Bergson, H. (1994) *The Creative Mind: An Introduction to Metaphysics*. New York: Citadel, p. 12.
8. Bergson, H. (2001) *Time and Free Will*. New York: Dover, first published in English in 1913, p. 38.
9. Hemingway, E. (2004) By line: Ernest Hemingway. In Phillips, L. (ed.) *Ernest Hemingway on Writing*. New York: Scribner, p. 139.
10. Woolf, V. (1981) In A. Olivier Bell (ed.) *The Diary of Virginia Woolf: Vol. 2 1920–1924*. London: Penguin, p. 158.
11. Woolf, V. (1981) In A. Olivier Bell (ed.) *The Diary of Virginia Woolf: Vol. 2 1920–1924*. London: Penguin, p. 308.
12. Fugard, A. (1983) In M. Benson (ed.) *Notebooks of Athol Fugard: 1960–1977*. London: Faber, p. 116.
13. Delbanco, A. (1999) The decline and fall of literature. *The New York Review of Books* 46(17), 4 November 1999.
14. J. Paul Hunter goes much further than this suggestion, and argues that professional critics adopted a mode of consumption and engagement that was detrimental. He outlines this in his book *Before Novels: The Cultural Contexts of Eighteenth Century Fiction* (New York: Norton, 1990) when he says 'Attacks on intention, accounts of the death of the author, anxieties about textual stability and its power to represent anything beyond itself, hostility toward any attempt to historicise a text or even admit its own cultural basis, and elevation of the critical over the creative faculty – all these conventions of mid- to late twentieth century criticism (some formalist, some structuralist, some post-structuralist) have a common tendency. They try to elevate the text itself and to give the critic special proprietary (priestly) power than ordinary readers (the laity) cannot achieve without going through rites of passage that involve dextrous intraverbal acts and monuments determined by those who own texts and determine how they are to be used. This privatising strategy

for texts now seems, fortunately, to be on the wane, but whatever its present status it has done major damage to any sense of a reading community, making "professional" readers arrogant and amateur ones defensive' (p. xii).
15. Turnovsky, G. (2003) The Enlightenment literary market: Rousseau, authorship, and the book trade. In *Eighteenth-Century Studies*, 36(3), 401–402.

Chapter 2
Acts and Actions of Creative Writing Can Be Observed in Finished Works?

1.

In universities and colleges during the 20th century, finished works of Creative Writing were most often the starting point for the examination of Creative Writing. By volume, that is; but also by inclination in a period in which cultural commodities were part of a rigorous centralised trade, intersecting, or sometimes running parallel, with a centralised commercial commodity market of considerable reach and depth. Finished works of Creative Writing were the starting point for a consideration of Creative Writing but also of creative writers, sometimes by inference, sometimes by direct association with works produced, sometimes in terms of conceptual links made between artefact and creator of the artefact, sometimes by cultural, chronological, aesthetic or personal association.

This list could go on, because in starting with a highlighting of finished works, both in the formal, professionalised approaches to Creative Writing and in a general commodity ideal of Creative Writing (supported by such notions as copyright, attached to ownership of tradable commodities, almost entirely of a completed kind) observation was drawn to one, often seen as primary, outcome of Creative Writing. Thus it was essential to suggest that the discovery of the acts and actions of creative writers could be made through a consideration of these works. Not to suggest this would have been tantamount to suggesting that Creative Writing mysteriously just happened.

Of course, this was not the strategy and we perhaps see this most obviously in the work of biographical critics. The notion that the acts and actions of creative writers could be discovered in their final works provided substantial underpinning to such analyses – recalling that the definition of 'action' used here is 'a collection of acts, sometimes joined by logic, intuition or fortuitous circumstance' and the definition of act is 'something done'. This from David Marr's excellent biography of Nobel Prize winner, Patrick White:

The Tree of Man, begun on the kitchen table, was finished on the new desk, its 'endless red linoleum top' usually hidden under a mess of paper . In White's house everything was bare, orderly and polished except for the surface of the desk. Above it hung the new de Maistre which had just arrived from London, one of Roy's *Descents from the Cross.*[1]

I've prefaced the comment on Marr's analysis with the word 'excellent' – because, of its genre, Marr's book is certainly excellent, an extremely good piece of biographical work. An award-winning biographer, Marr also had a closeness to the subject, Patrick White, and the life of his subject, to an extent all biographers could relate. So close was he that he writes of his involvement in the ceremony scattering the ashes of White's lover, Manoly Lascaris, some thirteen years after the death of White himself.

I held the plastic box while the poetry reader worked away at the lid with a knife. It popped open. We all looked in, as if we'd see something telling or unexpected there. I handed the box to Mobbs [Barbara Mobbs, White's literary executor]. She demurred briefly, then went to the edge and scattered a handful of ashes that fell straight to the bottom. The water was only a foot or so deep. We all took a turn and there was soon a carpet of white on the floor of the pool.[2]

Considering the importance of Lascaris, and indeed Mobbs, to White, there's little doubt in this simple, yet poignant moment of Marr's intimacy with the writer. There's little doubt either, in the tone and approach, that Marr takes in his biography of White or in his editing of White's letters,[3] that he has empathy with the life and the world he is describing. Rightly or wrongly in terms of what might be called 'critical distance', Marr is *within* the life of White, as much concerned with the creative writer as with writings; in fact, because this is biography, we could quite rightly say that by very definition Marr is concerned with the human aspects of his subject, even if the reason his work on White has been undertaken, can be undertaken, is because his subject is a famous creative writer whose finished work won awards and was (not to gloss the tensions of critical opinion) critically acclaimed.

So, finished works do occur in Marr's analysis and they are, as the earlier example exemplifies, tied more or less to the commentary that surrounds a period, or place, or event in Patrick White's life. In this broadly biographical sense Marr does present scenes and attitudes, White's discoveries and White's opinions, as components of White's finished works. Sometimes he does this directly, noting a particular observation that White made and later incorporated into one of his works of fiction, poems or plays. Other times, Marr speaks more generally, using what narratologically we might call 'summary' to build bridges in his story's chronology, to establish a general sense of cause and effect, and to maintain a trajectory to his White biography so that while the complexities of decision-making and free personal choice are not ignored, a sense of inter-relation of subject and theme is created. That is, Patrick White as subject and the wider thematic context of the famous, successful creative writer as the broad theme. And so:

> After a break at Kangaroo Island with the Duttons, White began to draft a long novel that had been working in his mind for years. Perhaps he put off writing 'The Binoculars and Helen Nell' too long. He might have begun before *The Solid Mandala* but felt he must first get Sarsaparilla out of his system. Then he put the novel off again to write the novellas for Geoffrey Dutton. Now in the New Year of 1966 he settled down to the task. He imagined that years of demanding and satisfying work lay ahead.[4]

The narrative structure of Marr's story is thus grounded. And White's life, likewise. Of course, we see here the difficulty of relating content and form, and of biographical work in itself. In what might well be seen as related comment, Harry Watson, reviewing Scott E. Caspar's *Constructing American Lives: Biography and Culture in Nineteenth Century America*, talks of the early 20th century's 'obsession with self' and suggests that there was a call for 'psychological explorations of personality that would satisfy readers' curiosity about famous people without engaging any public purpose whatsoever'[5]. Is Marr's focus also a psychological exploration? Is it part of the century's continued 'obsession with self'? Or is it, in opposition to Watson's comment on the early 20th century, aiming to serve a public purpose: in this case, the desire for the public to know more about a creative writer whose work has risen to considerable heights?

Perhaps it is all these things. But what, then, do we make of 'that had been working in his mind for years' and of 'he imagined that years of satisfying work lay ahead', and of 'he settled down to the task'? Certainly these are not analytical comments representing any deep psychological investigation. Nor do they seem to be obsessively focused on the 'self' of White; in essence, drawing the reader not to White's personality or to

White's life outside of Creative Writing but to some unstated set of actions that will now move White's creative enterprise onward.

And so, for the purposes of Marr's biography, White does indeed 'settle down to the task' – but not the task, that is, of Creative Writing *per se*, but the task of working in such a manner that will produce final works. Without this anchoring in certain kinds of activity, Marr's narrative loses its momentum. A skilled biographer, he needs his subject to have a recognisable public face, a material existence, and that material existence, for the creative writer represented, has to be grounded in *his works* not *his working*.

Let's make no mistake, Marr is entirely aware of the complex relationship between writing labour and writing output; or, to put it in earlier terms, of the complexities of creating in light of the artefacts that have valued after creation. He comments:

> After nearly ten years working on White, I needed a complete break. I refused invitations. I left seminars to academics. The last stop of my White career was a book tour of New Zealand that ended in a Timaru bookshop in 1994.[6]

This is not a cynical turn, merely the honest recognition by Marr that White is, regardless of any empathy or association Marr might feel, his biographer's subject. In being Marr's subject, and in relating as subject to the public outputs that have made him a likely success as a Marr's subject, White's life is placed in functional relief with his public, finalised works. This is all the more apparent when Marr struggles with new finds of largely unexpected White materials:

> I didn't rush down to look when White's letters poured into the National Library over the next decade, with little tributaries feeding into Sydney's Mitchell and Melbourne's La Trobe. I'd seen most of the material and a 644-page biography didn't need any fresh detail. But the Mobbs consignment to Canberra in 2006 broke my resolve. I was down there in a flash, working quietly with the librarians before the big public announcement, laughing and gnashing my teeth that the old bastard had kept so much from me. Up to a point, I understood what he was about [...].[7]

The question of whether final works of Creative Writing can reveal the acts and actions of Creative Writing is not answered by a turn to the biographers of creative writers, nor can it be answered by reference to biographical versus say 'textual' or 'cultural' criticism. Creative writers' acts and actions impact upon the results that emerge into the public sphere, and these final works observe a relationship determined at least partly by writerly choice and writerly intention. But the question remains: how important are they in uncovering what Creative Writing is?

2.

What this line of questioning is not trying to unearth is the dimensions and depths of 'literature'. Or, indeed, the nature of 'drama', the elementary aspects of 'film', the substance of any other artefact produced, or largely in existence, because of Creative Writing. It is not the aim here to define, or even investigate, what criteria we might use to speak of the final artefactual results of Creative Writing. And, in fact, not all artefacts that might be generated by Creative Writing are necessarily generated by Creative Writing. A film can come into existence without a script, a stage play likewise. A computer game, while certainly able to emerge from a creatively written text, might just as easily emerge from a designer's ideas interlinked by images set out on a storyboard. Creative Writing underpins its artefacts but it is not a substitute for them. Were this the case, then we could simply point toward the activities of creative writers and find there literature, drama, film ... But we cannot. What we find, alternatively, is Creative Writing. What emerges into the world as artefacts of creating, and is connected but not identical to the creating itself, emerges according to value systems that relate to such things as:

(1) variations of commercial and/or cultural commodification, throughout the world's cultures and throughout the world's history;
(2) the value placed on a particular creative writer's works (e.g. due to critical reception, or through other forms of notoriety, or because of the strength, or changes, of cultural perception that asks for further recognition).

The final works of creative writers, in this sense, take on the role of material exchange – but not simply of the materiality of written words themselves; rather the final works carry forth an *objectified* version of Creative Writing act and action, making human activity largely an *informer* of materiality. Creative Writing, in other words, is presented as object and in its very existence carries the *matter* of Creative Writing between writer and reader. There is a distinct difference here to notions of reification or concretism because this is not a case of an abstraction being considered concrete or of nature or 'divine will' being seen as the force behind creating. Rather, the fallacy relates to the role of ideas, the human mind, the imagination – which may best form the subject of further investigation.

For now, the acts and actions of Creative Writing, in the line of reasoning that relies on objectification, can indeed be observed in the final works of a creative writer. Here, for example, in relation to the Creative Writing of John Updike:

> In looking through Rabbit's [Harry 'Rabbit' Angstrom, the central character of Updike's 'Rabbit novels'] eyes, Updike explores the shifting boundaries of American identity during the postwar period. Changes in the fortunes of his characters, and in how they see themselves in relation to America, reflect Updike's evolving sense of his country.[8]

And, in response to questions of Updike's style:

> In examining the later Rabbit novels from the perspective of an increasing engagement with the outside world, however, it is important to acknowledge the inflections or limitations placed on this engagement by Updike's often-celebrated prose style. Any analysis of the thematic concerns of Updike's novels that fails to include the texture of his language as an object of critical inquiry risks over-looking the richly rewarding interpretations offered by examining the relationship between these two aspects of the Updike's writing.[9]

Two instances here, firstly in which character (not necessarily the creating of character) take on the aspect of changes in cultural condition, becoming iconic or physically representing 'boundaries', 'identity' in Updike's prose; and, secondly, in which style (not necessarily the adoption, employing or exploration of a style or styles) offers interpretative possibilities for a meeting with 'the outside world'. Materially, this bodes well because what Updike has delivered in his final works to the inter-preter is 'texture', an *'object* of critical enquiry'. The words chosen here do certainly carry metaphoric tones, but the author's meaning is literal. And the approach, while validly contributing to an investigation of literature, focusing strongly on final works, offers very little for a consideration of Creative Writing. Such approaches are common.

This on Jonathan Swift and *Gulliver's Travels*:

> One of the original illustrations of Gulliver's Travels shows an experimental word-processing machine (III.v.181). Swift guessed at the two satellites of Mars, and this machine satirizing 'speculative learning' appears to have anticipated the revolution that has come

to shape the lives of most people on earth – information retrieval systems, culminating in the ever-developing sophistication of computer technology, by which, in fact, this book was produced. Perhaps a resonant local irony may be pointed out.[10]

A wonderfully evocative piece of prose; but not joining Swift as creating individual and the holistic conditions of societal or cultural structures and/or functions, or indeed attempting to transgress historical time by suggesting common thematic conditions. Rather, aiming to initiate, or more accurately to 'anticipate', a dialogue between Swift (as creative writer) and Knowles (as informed critic). Interestingly, in this passage concentrating on the 'original illustrations' in the book. The result, thus, is based in another kind of exchange in which the final 'book' is the object of discussion and the subject is how books have also represented and shaped points of view. Additionally interesting that the discussion makes a direct link between 'printing' of books (the physical manifestation of Knowles' thoughts about the technological connections) and the 'ever-developing sophistication of computer technology', which at the time of Knowles' writing (the early/mid-1990s) had yet to be fully manifest in the extensive broadband adoption of the world wide web , the spread and strength of email use, the wider development of wireless computing (Wi-Fi) and ubiquitous mobile telephony – all of which have encouraged an almost global reconsideration of a chronology of creation and reception, and impacted upon a centralised commodity and culture market.

And for further consideration – this from mid-century critic, Arnold Kettle, in a book entitled *An Introduction to the English Novel*:

> This is an admirable example of Defoe's method. Utter verisimilitude is achieved by the insistence on detail: the precise financial calculations, the naming of the day of the week and the actual streets.[11]

'Method' and 'detail' here are entwined, with the accumulation of detail presented as an element of Defoe's truth telling strategic method. Kettle goes on to remark that 'it would not be quite true to say there is no pattern in Defoe's novels'.[12] We can perhaps wonder whether pattern in appearance equates with pattern in thought and, ultimately, with pattern in composition.

And this, further, in a lively journal article from Eugene O'Brien, exploring the influence of Yeats 'on Heaney's work':

> Both writers share an essentially postmodern project of unravelling the monological nationalist narrative of history and instead foregrounding

the aporias, antinomies and fault lines that have been glossed over by the sweep of historical narrative.[13]

And:

> Perhaps the most overt connection between these two poets is their winning of the Nobel prize for literature. In terms of their respective Nobel lectures, Yeats's *The Irish Dramatic Movement,* and Heaney's *Crediting Poetry,* there is a symphysis of thought in connection with the role that is played by the aesthetic in the realm of the political. Both writers stress the political circumstances within which their art was created.[14]

A fine piece of connective work, but the answer to the question of whether the investigation of the final works of creative writers embodies an investigation of the acts and actions of creative writers is only made more remote by the accumulating into suggestions of a shared 'post-modern project', a bringing together under an umbrella of post-event theory, and further removed again by treating the political as a 'realm', as if it too was primarily an accumulative category, assuaging the difficulties of relating individual or personal history to holistic history. This is hardly O'Brien's fault; his interest is in the literary world of these two Irish writers and, by extension, in literature within the national context of Ireland itself. Umberto Eco reminds us what is involved here in his discussion of 'the empirical reader'.

> Empirical readers can read in many ways, and there is no law that tells them how to read, because they often use the text as a container for their own passions, which may come from outside the text or which the text may arouse by chance.[15]

The same, of course, can be said about the creative writer who is also a reader! But if the creative writer who is also a reader applies the empirical information they have accumulated, more or less over time, from experience and active observation, from the *doing* of Creative Writing as well as the reading of final works of literature (or, indeed, watching or listening, or otherwise consuming) final works produced by Creative Writing then post-event knowledge is matched by the knowledge of the event (acts and actions) of Creative Writing. They may, or may not, be effective critics of literature, drama, film... but their involvement as readers emphasises that final works in themselves do not offer observations of the acts and actions of creative writers.

Notes

1. Marr, D. (1992) *Patrick White: A Life*. Sydney: Vintage, p. 297.
2. Marr, D. (2008) Patrick White: The Final Chapter. *The Monthly* 33, April 2008.
3. Marr, D. (1996) *Patrick White Letters*. Chicago: University of Chicago.
4. Marr, D. (1992) *Patrick White: A Life*. Sydney: Vintage, p. 457.
5. Watson, H. (2000) Review: Lies and Times: the changing genre of biography. In *Reviews in American History* 28(1), 48.
6. Marr, D. (2008) Patrick White: The Final Chapter. *The Monthly* 33, April 2008.
7. Marr, D. (2008) Patrick White: The Final Chapter. *The Monthly* 33, April 2008.
8. Colgan, J.P. (2002/2003) Going it alone but running out of gas: America's borders in John Updike's 'Rabbit' novels. *Irish Journal of American Studies* 11/12, 73.
9. Colgan, J.P. (2002/2003) Going it alone but running out of gas: America's borders in John Updike's 'Rabbit' novels. *Irish Journal of American Studies* 11/12, 75.
10. Knowles, R. (1996) *Gulliver's Travels: The Politics of Satire*. New York: Twayne, p. 105.
11. Kettle, A. (1962) *An Introduction to the English Novel, Volume One: To George Eliot*. London: Arrow, p. 63.
12. Kettle, A. (1962) *An Introduction to the English Novel, Volume One: To George Eliot*, London: Arrow, p. 63.
13. O'Brien, E. (2005) The anxiety of influence: Heaney and Yeats and the place of writing. *Nordic Irish Studies* 4, 119.
14. O'Brien, E. (2005) The anxiety of influence: Heaney and Yeats and the place of writing. *Nordic Irish Studies* 4, 126.
15. Eco, U. (1995) *Six Walks in Fictional Woods*. Cambridge (MA): Harvard University Press, p. 8.

Chapter 3

No Unfinished Works are Created by Creative Writers?

1.

On first sighting, plainly a ridiculous question! Are creative writers, therefore, destined to be some of the few in the world who always finish every single thing they have started? Probably a laudable life plan; but potentially somewhat unwieldy. On the other hand, reading the question in another way, could it be said no work of Creative Writing is ever truly finished? This recalls the adage attributed to Leonardo da Vinci, and later adapted and adopted by others, that 'art is never finished, only abandoned.' This is a slightly more palatable suggestion, though one that raises the spectre of a life of dissatisfaction or, at least, a life struggling for contentment.

If no work of Creative Writing is ever truly 'finished' do creative writers have any sense of achievement at all – one abandonment after another, each haunting the next and, where works are created in parallel, some sense that they, each one of them, has a half-life, seeking more attention than the one beside it so that it might be given the full life of finality? Again, this presents a picture of a purgatory, as if the creative practitioner must be punished for ever having attempted to be creative at all. So while it is palatable to accept that Creative Writing is sometimes (quite frequently even) the subject of the same time and life restraints that impact on most of us, and therefore some final works of Creative Writing are only offered up for dissemination because time or money or, quite simply, the human energy to expend on their undertaking has run out it is not so convincing that creative writers live their lives this way. A less extreme version might thus be, in this sense, that no works begun by creative writers are ever left 'unfinished'? They are, in essence, 'done with'. Something linked to Lorrie Moore's comment that 'in discussing writing one shouldn't set the idea of inspiration aside and speak only of hard work. Of course writing is hard work – or a very privileged kind of hard work.'[1] This might be worth investigating.

There is, however, a third alternative, and one that bears some clear and more concerted consideration. That is, that creative writers do not create only finished works. That, in an approach to exploring what Creative Writing is, where the disseminated artefacts, the commodities of commercial or cultural hegemony, the objects that bear the identities of other cultural foundations – those of moments in the history of publishing, or those in moments of the history of education, or those of cultural or aesthetic movements, of politics, economics, fame or infamy – that in such an approach a recognition of the *range* and, to the extent that a macro-study is limited only by space, the *purpose* of the works creative writers produce.

2.

> With me, though, the ambition to be a writer was for many years a kind of a sham. I liked to be given a fountain pen and a bottle of Waterman ink and new ruled exercise books (with margins), but I had no wish or need to write anything; and didn't write anything, not even letters: there was no one to write them to. [...] And though I liked new books as physical objects, I wasn't much of a reader.[2]

A recollection of his early writing or, perhaps as the writer suggests, 'non-writing' from the very highly regarded V.S. Naipaul. What constitutes *beginning* Creative Writing – whether broadly or in terms of specific projects – and *ending* Creative Writing is intriguing. Isak Dinesen comments:

> No, I really began writing before I went to Africa, but I never once wanted to be a writer. I published a few short stories in literary reviews in Denmark when I was twenty years old, and the reviews encouraged me, but I didn't go on – I don't know, I think I had an intuitive fear of being trapped.[3]

And Umberto Eco:

> I had started writing before the war, independently of the war. As an adolescent I wrote comic books, because I read lots of them, and fantasy novels set in Malaysia and Central Africa. I was a perfectionist and wanted to make them look as though they had been printed, so I wrote them in capital letters and made up title pages, summaries, illustrations. It was so tiring that I never finished any of them. I was at that time a great writer of unaccomplished masterpieces [...][4]

Nadine Gordimer recalls:

> [...] between the ages of fifteen and twenty, I was really teaching myself how to write – I had been writing, without the ability of self-criticism yet developed – since I was nine years old [...][5]

Nadine Gordimer's comments here are in an edited collection of comments by writers on the books they love. She talks in this section about Marcel Proust, remarking that:

> I have read and re-read *À la recherche du temps perdu* again and yet again, finally in the French original, and it speaks to me perhaps as no other novel does.[6]

The relationship between Creative Writing and reading is a productive place to consider how creative writers may begin to imagine themselves as creative writers, if indeed they ever imagine themselves this way. Might this have any connection with when they began writing creatively? What kinds, what modes of reading and, most importantly, *what reading* needs to inform that consideration?

How many interviewers have ever thought to ask a creative writer if they read the faces of friends, relatives, perfect strangers? How many creative writers read the weather, the tides, the temperature? How many read an email, a postcard, a newspaper, a television show, a website, a film? How many read a situation? The word 'reading' means, broadly, 'examining meaning'. It relates to receiving and, sometimes, often, with every good will, comprehending. It can mean to gain knowledge from something, to examine and decide upon intention. It's about discerning, attempting to grasp, interpreting. Naturally, creative writers are drawn to finished works of Creative Writing, not least because they do seek out material evidence of their own desired results, and they do seek out comparators, points of similarity and difference, shared ideas and ideals – novelists and poets drawn to literature, for example; screenwriters drawn to read films; playwrights to plays. Flannery O'Connor writes:

> 8 November '58
>
> I have never read any Japanese writers myself. Right now I am reading the Pasternak. It really is something. Also a travel book on Greece by Henry Miller. Never read any Henry Miller before but this book is very fine. Also reading a book called *The Eclipse of God* by Martin Buber that Dr Spivey sent me.[7]

And, on the same day, to Cecil Dawkins (a woman who was a fellow creative writer and a college teacher): 'This is the best story [The Mourner] you've sent me in every way.'[8] How many kinds of reading are there related on this one day, and in just these simple passages, alone? O'Connor receives, discerns, interprets – and the reading that occurs goes well beyond the works with which she is interacting. She is also interpreting how she should react in light of what kind of reading, and to what purpose.

It is fascinating, then, that anyone should ever consider that reading might be a narrowly defined activity or, indeed, that creative writers (because they write) limit what they read to things that are written. If we locate the beginnings of a creative writer's interest in Creative Writing, at least somehow, in some kind of exchange between many forms of reading and a decision to undertake Creative Writing then we might also ponder what kind of reading stimulates the urge to write creatively. *Beginning* Creative Writing, *undertaking* Creative Writing and, as sometimes is the case, *ending* Creative Writing.

On the relationship between reading and the *ending* of Creative Writing, Christine Brooke-Rose approaches this in two works, one of Creative Writing and one about Creative Writing. In the first, *Life, End Of*:

> [...] Except once, when Barbara goes out for a walk and the conversation turns to writing. This writing. Another ailment in fact.
> Writing. Now at an end, in both practice and theory, since the desk or computer position is too cardo-vasco de Hamer, lacerating the chest. But secretly taken up again after discovering the comfortable way of using the armchair, for the joy of bristling up words again. Just for fun. And perhaps therapy. Or here in bed, more precarious with just the board and no chair-arms. The text is described, owned up to rather. After all Tim is an ex-editor, so it feels quite natural. Two doubts are mentioned, (a) and (b) the most visible themes: are they a bore? Is the treatment light enough? He listens intently. Or does he? Shyly the question is asked. There are only five chapters or sections, would he read them down in the guest-room? Of course.[9]

In *Invisible Author: Last Essays*, she begins:

> Have you ever tried to do something very difficult as well as you can, over a long period, and found that nobody notices? That's what I've been doing for over thirty years [...]
> By 'very difficult' I don't mean difficult for the reader to read but difficult for the author to write. In theory, at any rate, the end result of

the specific constraints I shall be discussing should be invisible as such; in practice (otherwise the author wouldn't do it) it does alter the text read by the reader, who feels it as unfamiliar and for that reason alone drops it, dismisses it, the pleasure of recognition being generally stronger than the pleasure or puzzlement of discovery.[10]

Brooke-Rose displaying some elements of sadness and some elements of determination, equally, as she contemplates not where Creative Writing begins but where it ends, not least her own. The question nevertheless remains, once commenced, and before concluded, what *actual* works do creative writers produce?

3.

Creative Writing doesn't begin at the end. Creative Writing doesn't begin where it stops. Let me state this less enigmatically. *Creative Writing doesn't begin at the point at which a creative writer ceases to do it.* This is the case whether we are talking about a life of Creative Writing or about individual acts and actions of Creative Writing, acts and actions that may ultimately result in one or more final or completed works.

What occurs in the acts and actions of Creative Writing produces works, though not all of them are final. In fact, very few of them are final. That is not to say that creative writers spend their lives frustrated by the fact they can never finish anything. Rather, creative writers spend their lives perceiving and conceiving, and in that perceiving and conceiving, creating evidence of their activities, only some of which is disseminated, or even intended for dissemination. Much of this evidence consists of unfinished materials – that is, materials that have no aim of completion or, more accurately, works that relate in a complementary way to other activities being undertaken by the creative writer which may or may not have finality in mind.

We can thus say that Creative Writing consists of several levels of 'unfinished' activity, if indeed all of these activities were intended to be finished in the sense of producing a final artefact – which is highly unlikely – as well as some activities producing finished works. In all cases we can break this down into interconnected areas:

pre-working and pre-working evidence;

(1) complementary working – and complementary evidence;
(2) final works – works that may or may not be disseminated;
(3) post-works and post-working – which may be the pre-working for future Creative Writing.

In general, definition of these interconnected activities suggests goals. For example, the goal of investigation or the goal of composition, the goal of honing or advancing the quality of an artefact, the goal of completion, or the goal of speculation on a future Creative Writing activity or activities. We could replace the word 'goal' with 'ambition' or 'intention'. Either way, these are not entirely random activities, nor are they entirely structured or formed. The acts and actions that make them are fluidly representational of the psychological and physical variedness of the activity of Creative Writing itself. And yet, without the operation of perception and conception, much of the life of a creative writer would consist of no Creative Writing at all. In other words, creative writers live for much of their lives – at least as long as they are writing – in a constant state of perceiving and conceiving of works that may, at some point, become final artefacts of Creative Writing. But they also perceive of other things that have a symbiotic relationship with their Creative Writing, and they also conceive pieces of writing that work in complementary, supportive or obliquely connected ways with their core acts and actions. Creative writers also, as an aspect of Creative Writing, engage in what could rightly be located under the category of 'memory', not only memory of past working and past works, but also of things they have read, have discerned, interpreted, attempted to comprehend; that is: read, in the widest possible sense of what reading means.

With this in mind, definitions of Creative Writing can thus include **pre-working and pre-working evidence**. These are the kinds of activities that cannot easily be talked about as conclusive, yet they can be decisive. Note taking, for example. Scribbles, doodles, information gathering that might form texts or simply form notions. Reading: all kinds. Gathering evidence. Considering. Dreaming. Contemplating. Remembering. Visiting. Some plan. Some take a holiday. Pre-working produces evidence of many kinds, and is to be considered in terms of the acts and actions it involves but also can found in the evidence it produces, sometimes stated, sometimes recorded, sometimes observed, sometimes easy to discover, sometimes incredibly difficult.

Complementary working, and complementary evidence, is that which occurs while a creative writer is working. This could be seen in a 'life story' way – that is, the long term history of a creative writer's working life, in part a chronology of core works that have emerged ('core' meaning the primary works that a creative writer felt they were working on at any given time). It can, thus, have some connection with dissemination in that a creative writer may consider their primary activities those connected with works they (or others) will disseminate. Complementary working can also relate to 'large' and 'smaller' projects – in other words, a creative writer might be working on a long piece of writing but also complete shorter or smaller works along the way. It can also be that creative writers are doing, and writing, other things and these too can impact on Creative Writing and form part of the complementary evidence of the acts and actions being undertaken. The relationship between complementary and core activities and complementary and core artefacts offers a great deal of support for how Creative Writing is fluid and interconnected, relating to the indivisibility of activities that Henri Bergson talks about, and to the influences of exertion and animation that he likewise propounds.

Ultimately, the creative writer may produce **final works (works that may or may not be disseminated)**. These final works may be final for the creative writer, but not for other individuals receiving these works (for example, an editor or a publisher). They may be final, and yet feel to the creative writer as if they require more working, more action – but time, or money or energy or motivation or some other factor prevents the creative writer continuing. They may, in this sense, be 'complete' but not 'final'. Whatever the case, these tend to be the works – whether in the study of literature or other art forms such as drama, film, music – these tend to be the works that are primarily studied, the starting points for the post-event analysis (that is, analysis after the event of creating) that seeks to interpret the artefacts and, as can be the case, sometimes includes in that interpretation some consideration of the creative writer, the creative writer's actions and/or the environment and context of the creative writer's activities.

But neither Creative Writing nor the artefacts generated by Creative Writing, paradoxically, stop at 'final' works. **Post-works and post-working (which may be the pre-working for future Creative Writing)** include the creative writer's own commentaries on their work – verbally, textually, formally (e.g. readings, presentations, discussions, interviews) or informally (e.g. casual emails, conversations with friends). Post-working also includes reading and re-reading the final work. Others may engage with the creative writer in post-working so that post-event analysis, criticism produced either by those seeking to review the work for the literary press or those examining the work for longer-term academic purposes may produce post-works which may or may not impact on the creative writer. A creative writer's post-working, also, might be the foundations on which new Creative Writing begins and any division between previous and new acts and actions – that is post-working and pre-working – may be blurred by the relationship that any act or action can have with any other act or action. In addition, the presence of an artefact (whether that artefact is, for example, notes relating to a final work or some information pertaining to a future work; whether it is a completed piece of work or a mere doodle of a notion that might form the crux of another exploration) may impact on this relationship, and that includes artefacts which seem, or are, vastly removed from the Creative Writing at hand. In some way, then, it might be said that all Creative Writing involves complementary acts and actions rather than pre-working and post-working, and yet this would be to downgrade the status of final works entirely, and we return to the notion that creative writers live lives devoted to incompleteness. This suggestion defies commonsense. Rather, post-working and post-works can take structured or unstructured forms, finished works and unfinished works, evidence in support of conception, perception and memory, and the relationship between post-working and post-works and pre-working and pre-works is one of the bases on which creative writers continue to be creative writers. That is, to return to earlier: once begun, Creative Writing continues until it stops. It doesn't begin when it ends; but, equally it must be happening for it to be Creative Writing.

Many unfinished works are thus created by creative writers. And in the acts and actions they create many works, of many kinds, many of which necessarily have the status of being such things as incomplete, fragmentary, momentary, ephemeral, personal, speculative, as well as works that are (or sometimes only 'seem') finished. Creative Writing, being an activity, is not defined by finality[11] – except in the sense that creative writers can cease to undertake it.

Notes

1. Moore, L. (2001) Interviewed by E. Gaffney. *The Paris Review* 158, Spring-Summer 2001, 57.
2. Naipaul, V.S. (2000) *Reading and Writing: A Personal Account*. New York: New York Review of Books, p. 4.
3. Dinesen, I. (1956) Interviewed by E. Walker. *The Paris Review* 14, Autumn 1956, 11.
4. Eco, U. (2008) Interviewed by L. A. Zanganeh. *The Paris Review* 185, Summer 2008.
5. Gordimer, N. (2000) In R. B. Schwarz (ed.) *For the Love of Books: 115 Celebrated Writers on the Books They Most Love*. New York: Berkeley, p. 103.
6. Gordimer, N. (2000) In R. B. Schwarz (ed.) *For the Love of Books: 115 Celebrated Writers on the Books they Most Love*. New York: Berkeley, p. 103.
7. O'Connor, F. (1979) In S. Fitzgerald (ed.) *The Habit of Being: The Letters of Flannery O'Connor*. New York: Vintage, p. 302.

8. O'Connor, F. (1979) In S. Fitzgerald (ed.) *The Habit of Being: The Letters of Flannery O'Connor.* New York: Vintage, p. 302.

9. Brooke-Rose, C (2006) *Life, End Of.* Manchester: Carcanet, p. 59.

10. Brooke-Rose, C. (2002) *Invisible Author: Last Essays.* Columbus: Ohio University Press, p. 1.

11. We could even say that speculation on Creative Writing and what it might produce is a constant dynamic, both mental and physical. Writing in the online *New Yorker*, Andrea Walker in 'The Book Bench', quotes creative writer Lev Grossman as saying:

> A note about my writing desk. It is wobbly and made of wood, and came into my life when my girlfriend dragged it in from the curb one day. In short, it is a piece of crap. A few weeks ago, I bought a truly beautiful table from a flea market to replace it. It's a huge metal-topped industrial work bench that someone had salvaged from an abandoned factory in Pennsylvania and fixed up. But it turns out that it's too heavy to carry up the stairs, and if it weren't too heavy it would still be too big to fit through the door of my study. I often fantasize about the masterpieces I would write if I could only get that workbench out of my landlord's foyer. (28 August 2000)

http://www.newyorker.com/online/blogs/books/?xrai
Accessed 30.8.09.

Chapter 4

All Works of Creative Writing are Disseminated?

1.

No doubt we will each readily agree that the above question can be answered in the negative. Already, it has been ventured that many works produced by creative writers do not get disseminated, do not have any purpose for the creative writer in being disseminated, are not seen by those dealing in the sale of the outputs of creative writers as artefacts for dissemination, and yet are crucial to Creative Writing.

All works of Creative Writing are simply not intended as public documents. And yet, in certain circumstances connected with cultural commodification or, more broadly, because of a human appreciation of Creative Writing or of a certain creative writer or writers, evidence of Creative Writing which would not normally become public does become public. The relationship between acts and actions and works is considerably complicated here by the intersection of societal considerations as well as individual ones. If the proposition 'Creative Writing involves a set of activities, or process that can be discovered by the investigation of disseminated works of Creative Writing', and not all works of Creative Writing are disseminated, then how accurate can any discovery be that relies on disseminated artefacts?

Firstly, then, the role of public cultural bodies becomes notable. Written in a rollicking fashion by Leslie Hotson, and published in *ELH: The Journal of English Literary History*, in 1942, the sense of the literary detective is strong in the following piece, and the efforts to unearth private communications to enhance the knowledge of the publicly disseminated artefacts of Creative Writing, makes for a very fine tale:

> No doubt success and immunity here made me foolhardy; for when I attempted the same sort of thing [as his investigations regarding Christopher Marlowe] with the lost letters of Shelley to his wife Harriet, I got a scare that will last me a long time. A pure chance led me to the copies of these long-sought and priceless letters hidden

away in an obscure corner of the Chancery records; and by the way, it was here that I first ran into the commercial side of the Legal Room that I mentioned. For the Shelley letters date from 1816. They are therefore on the wrong side of the deadline, 1800, and are treated like any modern document which you pay for inspecting. I paid my thirty cents, and got nine hitherto unknown letters of Shelley's in return.[1]

The commercial and cultural wonders of the 'Records Office', 'the largest collection of national archives in the world,'[2] Chancery Lane, Lincoln's Inn, the 'Legal Room', the accoutres of nation and empire and identity. Solid evidence at a time of instability – the date of Hotson's article no mere thing. Great import lives here:

> The man who wishes to add to what we know about the background of Shakespeare would do better to devote his days to searching in Chancery Lane, than emulate the homely spider in drawing gossamer out of himself to spin a web of fancy about Francis Bacon, or the Earl of Oxford, or yet a literary committee of seven noblemen.[3]

History and ideas about cultural worth relate closely in the valuing of the private, or otherwise unlikely to be disseminated, outputs of creative writers. Other words enter the discussion, the word and concept of 'heritage' being of considerable note. Jamie Andrews, Head of Modern Literary Manuscripts at the British Library, offers some insight into collecting policy – that is, the way in which a large public organisation such as the British Library participates in creating routes of dissemination for outputs of Creative Writing that would otherwise be unseen.

> The kind of stuff we deal with has economic value and that is decided on the basis of comparators. With unique material it's not that easy to find those comparators. How do you compare a Beckett letter with a Pinter letter? However, what we're really concerned with is research value. We hope the budget will be there to purchase what we think is valuable for research. [...] some subjective knowledge and personal taste come into it, though it is backed by assessments of the research background in the UK and America, in terms of what's being taught in undergraduate and postgraduate study.[4]

Honest, pragmatic stuff. What more could a public institution do, given that the primary discussions of the past in relation to the study of literature have not necessarily been discussions about Creative Writing? And efforts have been made to preserve – certainly in more recent times – all those items of pre-works, complementary works and post-works that might relate to an appreciation of the final works of certain creative writers and certain Creative Writing:

> Almost everything that is unique is considered [...] when we look at archives we're looking at how each piece relates to the others. Each is not an individual item in the way that printed books are a succession of individual items. An archive is an undivided whole in which every single item adds value to the others, from the pristine quality drafts to the odd scrap of paper.[5]

Again, there's no pretence here, no cultural cover-up. The British Library's role is to preserve and promote the heritage of Britain, and to do so in relation to literature the Library has policies that define its interests and practices, as well as referring to the 'personal tastes' of its acknowledged experts. Given financial restraints, as well as space constraints, and in light of the remit of the Library, could it do anything other than reflect a preference for Creative Writing defined according to final works and limited to creative writers whose role in British culture has been formally acknowledged in the academic study of literature (and, of course, drama, to an extent, film and so on)?

And yet, how accurate a reflection of Creative Writing is the British Library's archival collection? Has it ever purported to be? There is not space here to debate the nature of collecting policy at libraries throughout the world. Maybe, simply to recall, in passing, comments on the creation of a 'Catholic Library for Dublin' that 'the Irish title chosen for it, *Leabharlann an Chreidimh* (Library of the Faith) epitomises its character.'[6] All libraries, and their archives, are in some sense libraries of faith – their characters are epitomised by a faith in a certain way of observing, reading, preserving, and presenting the worlds in which they operate. The British Library has done much to raise the interest in Britain's literary heritage but its remit is not to point the way to the Creative Writing of each British citizen who chose, or chooses, to write creatively. Its wider purpose as a public institution is not to collect, disseminate, or provide support for dissemination, of the evidence of Creative Writing left behind by those who – for whatever reason – are not considered important to preserving the holistic concept of a 'picture of Britain's literary heritage'.

This is not a criticism of the British Library, rather a simple statement of the nature of the faith and intention of such a public institution. It is 'not just preserving the works of the greatest writers in Britain' but 'an over all view of our heritage'.[7] But, of course, the sense of 'heritage' being used here is not individual but national, not centred on the personal but on the nature of a social community. And yet, is it not the personal where most Creative Writing dwells, in the private world of creative writers, only a small portion of who find their final works received in such way that anyone would seek out any private evidence of creation that might reveal something of the nature of the Creative Writing and the specific creative writer?

To keep at least a balance, all this of course is not merely relative to the collecting, preservation, and dissemination policies of the British Library. The Director of the Harry Ransom Center at the University of Texas at Austin expresses similar ideals:

> The Ransom Center is indeed a fine institution, but I believe that the most exciting years are yet to come. We continue to expand and deepen our twentieth-century collections, acquiring the archives of major figures – such as Norman Mailer and David Mamet – who will likely form the foundation of culture in the next century.[8]

'The foundation of culture', 'heritage', 'major figures', 'the kind of stuff we deal with has economic value': there is purpose and reason here but the aim is not to ensure (and it does not ensure) that works of Creative Writing, or evidence of Creative Writing, is made available for this and future generations. Nor is the aim of these public institutions that preserve and disseminate the results of Creative Writing without recourse to public imperatives. Thus here, all works of Creative Writing are not disseminated. Indeed, all works of literature, all works of art, are not disseminated. But how does this then relate to discoveries about the art of Creative Writing?

2.

No, oddly enough I've written my last several novels in longhand first. I had an enormous, rather frightening stack of pages and notes for *The Assassins*, probably eight hundred pages – or was it closer to a thousand? It alarms me to remember. *Childwold* needed to be written in longhand, of course. And now everything finds its initial expression in longhand and the typewriter has become a rather alien thing – a thing of formality and impersonality. My first novels were all written on a typewriter, first draft straight through, then revisions, then final draft. But I can't do that any longer.

The thought of dictating into a machine doesn't appeal to me at all. Henry James's later works would have been better had he resisted that curious sort of self-indulgence, dictating to a secretary. The roaming garrulousness is usually corrected when it's transcribed into written prose.[9]

Joyce Carol Oates, when asked whether she'd ever considered composing her work by 'dictating into a machine'. There's so much in this passage that points to, if not entirely exposes, the way Oates thinks of her Creative Writing. The question she asks – asks herself mostly – about the size of the stack of pages and notes for *The Assassins*. Does it matter? It appears it does, in some way, to Oates. Or, alternatively, is this a way of conveying some aspect of the labour she wishes acknowledged in her choice of Creative Writing as a career? Is it that 'expression' for Oates is something different, some other act, than say 'organisation' or 'refine-ment', to choose a few random ideals? The point she makes about impersonality.

So what are the physical and psychological links that Joyce Carol Oates makes while engaging in Creative Writing and how does the action of writing in longhand support those links while the typewriter does not? And the word 'formality' – what's this? Further, for a creative writer who works in academe, what might this mean? The sequential suggestion she makes – 'first draft straight through, then revisions, then final draft'. Is this how she works, or how she finds it best to imagine her working, or how she chooses to present her working? And the criticism of Henry James? Is this in the vein of a post-event criticism – that James's final works don't appear to her to have the same quality that his earlier works display? A personal opinion or a shared literary critical point-of-view? Or is this an event-based criticism in which she is criticising the act of dictating in Creative Writing and, not ignoring the consideration of the final works themselves, is this then a little more about how she views the notion of 'self-indulgence' than about the final works themselves? James's Creative Writing habits are not something that have gone un-noticed by other creative writers, with Cynthia Ozick's playful novella *Dictation* (2008)[10] envisaging a meeting between the stenographers of Henry James (Theodora Bosanquet) and Joseph Conrad (Lilian Hallowes). Here's how Theodora Bosanquet appears in James's own pocket diary:

18 October 1912 Friday
Have been up more – dictating letters to Miss Bosanquet in a.m. – till 1.30. The Protheros gone. Have signed lease of 21 Carlyle Mansions. Better, but great pain very obstinate; very poor time.

19 October 1912 Saturday

Miss Bosanquet ill and absent.
Called on her at Bradleys.

20 October 1912 Sunday

Miss B. ill and absent. Went again in afternoon to ask.

21 October 1912 Monday

Begins 4th week of illness. Continuance of great local pain and bad nights.

25 October 1912 Friday

Miss Bosanquet left for 10 days.[11]

James himself was also ill during this time (thus the entry on 21 October) with an attack of *herpes zoster*, shingles, that is said to have lasted through until 1913.[12] There's something of the relationship between Theodora Bosanquet and James revealed here, even if only in the clear sense of James's urgency and what might be called, perhaps, 'employer-employee' relations; but, of course, Bosanquet was herself a writer and editor, later literary editor of *Time and Tide*. Here is a 1937 review by Theodora Bosanquet of Virginia Woolf's *The Years*:

> Did she, putting her ear to an acoustically curved shell, hear a voice, the assembled voice of other English novelists, murmuring: 'Now it's your turn. You who have tossed time about like a shuttlecock, disdained and defied the tolling of the hours, come off that lofty cloud. Let the years pass in the order of their chronological procession. Bridge your abysses in something more like the ordinary manner'?
>
> Whether she asked that voice, or whether she just wanted to assure herself that any form can be sufficiently exploited by a sufficiently intelligent and accomplished writer, there can be no doubt that Mrs Woolf has brought off her trick.[13]

At each juncture, from that which brings Joyce Carol Oates into critical collision with Henry James, to that which initiates a 'meeting' between Theodora Bosanquet and Cynthia Ozick, to that which brings Virginia Woolf into the daily life of Theodora Bosanquet there is an *association of event*, the event of Creative Writing, in which various works emerge, some shared and some not shared, some private, some public, some made public. But the junctures themselves, while sometimes incorporating cornerstone materials borne out of a varied textual, material history, are brought about because of a shared creativity which vitalises and informs their responses to each other. It is this that generates junctures.

3.

Creative Writing creates numerous works, most often remaining in the hands of the creative writer without organisation or thought to preservation, or commercial or cultural value, if indeed they are kept at all. Other times these works become part of the writer's own garnering, a collection of artefactual evidence that is somehow accumulated or even actively collected, sometimes in relation to specific works, sometimes in relation to specific periods, or sometimes merely on the basis of entirely fortuitous timing (for example, the organisational fervour of a house move or the virtual filing away of materials left on an old computer, or the curious ferreting together of materials brought about by turn of nostalgia, or the specific need to recall information for further Creative Writing of some kind). Occasionally these works are accumulated by others but still not distributed to a wider readership. This might occur if the creative writer shares some of their working, and some of their works, with family or with friends, with an editor or editors, with publishers or with agents, with other creative writers, with confidantes. Sometimes the works of creative writers are collected and preserved by public institutions, according to the public policies that impact on such institutions, and in line with largely holistic concerns associated with words such as 'heritage'. Heritage, here a connective concept in which social or cultural wholes are represented by the inclusion of individual and group outputs, evidence valued according to integration into an agreed typology. The relationship between creative writers' works, how they are valued or not valued, whether they are preserved or not preserved, and how they form exchanges, often relates to communication between an individual sense of ownership and significance and a cultural or societal sense of ownership and significance. 'The Author' in John Barth's often very humorous novel *Letters*, writes to a certain 'A. B. Cook IV':

> Dear Mr Cook,
>
> Actually, I am as dismayed as gratified by your long letters to me of a month ago and it even lengthier enclosures. Gratified of course by your ready response to my inquiry concerning your ancestors; by your providing me with copies of those remarkable letters from Andrew Cook IV to his unborn child; by your diverting account of

the subsequent genealogy down to yourself; by your supererogatory offer – nay, resolve – to enrich me yet further with the materials from abortive *Marylandiad*: the posthumous adventures, as it were, of A.B.C. IV. But dismayed, sir, by your misconstruction of my letter and by your breathtaking assertion that we collaborated on my *Sot-Weed Factor* novel – indeed, that we have any prior connection whatsoever![14]

'No prior connection whatsoever': how often might it be that Creative Writing is undertaken without prior connection? Rather, the Creative Writing remains with the creative writer, in the gathering of materials to inform a work or works, in the comparisons, the juxtapositions of evidence, in the notes, the exploring of ideas in words, images, sounds. The drafting, attempts to create, speculative investigation of form or style ...

In 1953, nine years before his death, William Faulkner wrote '[...] now I realise for the first time what an amazing gift I had: uneducated in every formal sense, without even very literate, let alone literary, companions, yet to have made the things I made [...]. I don't know why God or gods, or whoever it was, selected me to be the vessel.'[15] 'Working again on my mss, which ran dry on me at home in August, which may have been partly responsible for my [...] trouble. It's going alright now though.'[16] The 'gift', the 'vessel' running dry, is not one of his books wedged on a reef, to wildly extend this metaphor, but the Creative Writing that he is undertaking, and the various works that he sees, entirely not disseminated, right in front of him. He had, of course, been awarded the Nobel Prize for Literature four years previously.

Notes

1. Hotson, L. (1942) Literary serendipity. In *ELH* 9(2), June 1942, 91.
2. Hotson, L. (1942) Literary serendipity. In *ELH* 9(2), June 1942, 81.
3. Hotson, L. (1942) Literary serendipity. In *ELH* 9(2), June 1942, 92.
4. Andrews, J. (2009) Interview with G. Harper. In C. Sullivan and G. Harper (eds) *Authors at Work: The Creative Environment*. Cambridge: Brewer, p. 70.
5. Andrews, J. (2009) Interview with G. Harper. In C. Sullivan and G. Harper (eds) *Authors at Work: The Creative Environment*. Cambridge: Brewer, p. 71.
6. Brown, S.J. (1922) A Catholic library for Dublin. In *Studies: An Irish Quarterly Review* 11(42), June 1922, 307.
7. Andrews, J. (2009) Interview with G. Harper. In C. Sullivan and G. Harper (eds) *Authors at Work: The Creative Environment*. Cambridge: Brewer, p. 76.

8. Staley, T.F. (2009) Director of the Ransom Centre at The University of Texas at Austin. Director's Note. http://www.hrc.utexas.edu/about/director/. Accessed 14.8.09.
9. Oates, J.C. (1978) Interviewed by R. Phillips. In *The Paris Review*, Fall-Winter 1978, 3–4.
10. Ozick, C. (2008) Dictation. In *Dictation: a Quartet*. Boston: Houghton Mifflin Harcourt, p. 1.
11. James, H. (1988) In L. Edel and L.H. Powers (eds) *The Complete Notebooks of Henry James*. New York: OUP, p. 369.
12. Edel, L. and Powers, L.H. (eds) (1988) *The Complete Notebooks of Henry James*. New York: OUP, p. 350.
13. Bosanquet, T. (1997) Review of *The Years*. In *Time and Tide*, reprinted in R. Majumdar, A. McLaurin (eds) *Virginia Woolf*. London: Routledge, p. 367.
14. Barth, J. (1980) *Letters: a Novel*. London: Secker and Warburg, pp. 532–533.
15. Faulkner, W. (1977) To Joan Williams, Wednesday 29 April 1953. In J. Blotner (ed.) *Selected Letters of William Faulkner*. New York: Random House, p. 348.
16. Faulkner, W. (1977) To Malcolm A Franklin, Tuesday October 1953. In J. Blotner (ed.) *Selected Letters of William Faulkner*. New York: Random House, p. 354.

Chapter 5

All Dissemination of Creative Writing Occurs, and Has Occurred, Similarly?

1.

If not all 'works' of Creative Writing are disseminated – all 'outputs', 'artefacts', 'evidence', the inverted commas used here to suggest how we view these items requires some further discussion – if these are not all disseminated, but that *some* final works are disseminated, how then has this occurred? Books are perhaps the most obvious form widely associated with Creative Writing as final works, though the evolution of film, and then television, and then the new electronic media could easily suggest to us that books are not the form in which most 20th and 21st century readers/audiences have acquired the final works of creative writers. Quite the opposite, in fact. Inequalities associated with Creative Writing and the dissemination of works of Creative Writing have come in three clear forms: (1) inequalities of time and application in relation to the Creative Writing itself, involving such things as personal circumstance, 'group' circumstance (for example, family or social group, regional or national foci); (2) inequality in terms of dissemination of particular works of Creative Writing, so that works of a certain kind, type or form, works by certain creative writers by virtue of critical or cultural reception, works with a certain cultural or contemporary perspective, find themselves in greater favour at a given time and place; (3) inequality of reception of one or other form of these works, so that in any period the dissemination of one or other final form can raise questions of inequality of reader/audience attention. To take the 20th century as a case study:

The evolution of media in the 20th century brought about a number of reactions associated with such inequalities, not least those which questioned the impact of new forms on 'reading', even if the definitions of reading being adopted were in the first instance relatively narrow. For example, a 1951 study of the impact of television on school children, offered the observation that:

The child's role in relation to the mass media is essentially a passive one, whereas the other playtime behavior of children often involves highly active participation of the child in the real environment [. . .]. It has been widely reported that adults do less reading, movie-going and radio-listening after they acquire a TV than they did before, and the same seems to be true of children.[1]

The fear here that passivity separates the child from the 'real' is intriguing, further associating this separation specifically with television, while 'movie-going' and 'radio-listening' involve the activeness that is associated with 'reading'. The television is an object on two levels: the appliance itself, 'a TV', and the programmes that it offers as texts, which somehow create passivity. Films, however, are about the activity of 'going' and radio is about the activity of 'listening'.

Interestingly, all these forms remain objects to be interacted with – or, in the case of television, passively seated before, it seems. Rather than seeing the final forms as some artefactual evidence of a more extensive human creative activity they are considered as texts and the creative and critical engagement that brought them about is not referred to in the discussion of readership or audience. Surprisingly, that is, because this 1951 report is considering a clash between passivity and activity and a fixed sense of how these forms came about could never deal adequately with the question of human exchange. Bring the discussion forward fifty years and this is what occurs:

We found that girls read more frequently than boys in their leisure time; that reading scores are positively related to the frequency with which children read in their leisure time; that boys spend more time than girls watching TV and playing computer games; and that the frequency with which children read is negatively related to the time they spend watching TV and playing computer games [. . .]. Correlations between the time spent watching TV during the week and reading achievement are not significant. This finding may surprise. Children spend, on average, substantially more time watching TV than playing computer games, but despite this, the strength of the relationship between computer games and reading achievement is stronger.[2]

In 1951 the extent of the relationship with the 'real', the way this was said to be impacted upon by television and the relative degrees of activity and passivity were the primary concerns. In the later study, published in 2000, amounts of time devoted to consuming each form is the focus, as is the ways in which consuming one form impacts on time spent on consuming another.

All this might seem peripheral to a discussion of Creative Writing, but it should not, given the huge amount of material produced by creative writers that did, and does, find its way into film, television, and computer games. Similarly, as these studies of reading habits locate reading in the disseminated final works of creative writers they highlight the questionable notion that engagement with Creative Writing is fundamentally an engagement with objects, even if these objects are then themselves examined in relation to their presentation of words, images, sounds.

Historically, of course, books are most often seen to loom largest in the history of Creative Writing and changes in the way in which books have been produced and distributed reflect on how Creative Writing has been undertaken, received and considered more generally. John Brewer, considering English Culture in the 18th century, remarks:

> As the number of books increased and the system of their distribution grew, it became easier to find them. Books could be bought, hired or borrowed either from commercial establishments and institutions or from individuals. The humblest literature – chapbooks, cheap abbreviated novels, almanacs and ballads – could be bought from itinerant pedlars and chapmen who travelled the countryside selling reading matter, trinkets, gifts, household goods and toys.[3]

Add to this Mark Rose's comment:

> The point to be stressed is the difference between the system of cultural production and regulation characteristic of the sixteenth and seventeenth centuries and the later system that developed based on the idea of authorial property. For one thing, in the early modern period it was usual *to think of a text as an action*, not a thing.[4] [My emphasis]

The significance of the 18th century to changing views on Creative Writing, therefore, becomes even more obvious. To think of a text 'as a thing' most certainly allows for the kind of commodity cultures that flourished in the 20th century and creates a situation in which response to the object replaces response to the human involvement in its creation. This is not to say that the object is not significant – indeed, much can be made of the evidence of Creative Writing and of the activities of creative writers – but it is to say that if Creative Writing is presented as a substance, a material, then already most of it goes unnoticed, unacknowledged and, thus, unconsidered. This goes some way toward suggesting ways in which the acts and actions and the artefacts of Creative Writing came to be seen as occupying different spatial and temporal positions and how creative writers came to occupy the place of adjunct to the final artefacts that some of them released to the world.

Of course, those even casually familiar with theoretical exchanges that took place in second half of the 20th century in such academic areas as literary studies, cultural studies, semiotics, the analysis of language and communication – broadly within what has been called 'critical theory' – will recognise that the objectification of Creative Writing has another side. Philosopher and critic Roland Barthes writes:

> Classic criticism has never paid any attention to the reader; for it, the writer is the only person in literature. We are now beginning to let ourselves be fooled no longer by the arrogant antiphrastical recriminations of good society in favour of the very thing it sets aside, ignores, smothers, or destroys; we know that to give writing its future, it is necessary to overthrow the myth: the birth of the reader must be at the cost of the death of the Author.[5]

In some ways it didn't matter what the full extent of Barthes's argument really was, because the title, and later general adoption of his expression 'The Death of the Author', fitted perfectly with the notion of empowering consumers to treat writing as object, even if Barthes's more pressing intention was to promote the extension of how readership was viewed and considered and to explore the ways in which a piece of writing may contain many layers and many meanings. The creative writer, in this context, becomes associated with a 'tyranny' in which authority is located in the author and therefore a concentration on the author, most particularly on a singular authorial figure, limits the dimensions that might be explored in a text, and disempowers the audience whose impressions actually define the meaning of the text.

What Barthes inadequately addresses is the clash between materialism and idealism or, to be more specific, he brings together two sets of actions, gives the persons acting names such as author, 'scriptor' (Barthes view of the modern 'author' who is reduced to a combiner of pre-existing texts, and comes into being at the same time as the text, rather than existing before it) and reader and then locates the nexus of the discussion, regardless of the consciousness and minds working, in the physical object of the text. In this configuration, Creative Writing is not only validated as textual inscription and the human acts and actions that occur to produce it are misinterpreted as something to do with the ownership of works not of working. Nothing in Creative Writing could be further from the truth.

2.

Demonstrably, the discussion so far has been predicated on the idea that the question 'all dissemination of Creative Writing occurs, and has occurred, similarly?' relates to the dissemination of objects, whatever varieties and types these objects occupy. And yet, the argument that has previously been presented is that Creative Writing consists of human acts and actions and that the artefacts created – of which there are many, a great number of which are never disseminated, either because they are not intended to be disseminated or because particular cultural or commercial emphases don't support their dissemination – and the artefacts are merely elements of the activities that are Creative Writing.

With this in mind, it could be said that very little Creative Writing is disseminated at all; that Creative Writing lies in unrecorded action, the unseen movement of a pen or the private tapping on computer keys, in the creative writer's reading, with all that the term 'reading' covers, in the mindscapes of perception and conception, in the workings of a creative writer's memory, in the manifestations in physiological and psycho-logical dispositions, of the individual creative writer or team of creative writers. And that it is these we should be considering when considering how the dissemination of Creative Writing has occurred.

Along this line of reasoning, what then can be considered relates to action context, and this could include social structures as well as personal dispositions and intentions, cultural meanings and functions, personal and societal economic and political conditions, physical environments – both the micro elements of the creative writer's desk or home, the specific spaces of creation, and the macro environments of history, culture, society, geography, nation, for example; these, to list only a few possibilities.

Such considerations might broadly be labelled as 'constructivist'. That is, concentrating on the human choices of creative writers, as phenomena. They could, in addition, give productive further voice (in opposition to the suggestions made by Barthes) to the idea that the individual or group of individuals that is responsible for the acts and actions of Creative Writing are not imposing a limit on the texts that emerge from their activities; rather that the concentration on the text itself imposes such limits and, along with this, dehumanises the nature of Creative Writing. Individuals, or this group, is the focus here, generically labelled 'creative writer/s', though frequently the definition of either individual or group has found itself linked primarily to final works – so, 'the short story writer', 'poets', 'a screenwriter', 'she's a playwright', 'novelists'. Social constructivist thinking has been used to explore the actions of individuals and groups generally. In relation to the sciences, Karin Knorr-Cetina has explored this in relation to the 'manufacture of knowledge' in science, noting in her 1981 book:

> Laws proposed by science are transfactual and rule-like, rather than descriptively adequate. Thus the practical success of science depends more upon the scientists ability to analyse a situation as a whole, to think of several different levels at once, to recognise clues, and piece together, than upon the laws themselves.[6]

Along with:

> It is the scientist's knowledge of what is a problem and what counts as a solution, educated guesses about where to look and what to ignore, and highly selective expectation-based tinkering with the material that guides them toward an innovative result.[7]

And:

> Unrealized solutions are important to scientists as organizing principles for subsequent actions and selections.[8]

Further:

> The laboratory response was composed of hurried ad hoc decisions. [...] For every bit of published 'method' there seems to be a bit of unpublished know-how [...][9]

Replace the word 'scientist' with 'creative writer' and it becomes plain how such constructivist thinking can assist us in examining how Creative Writing occurs, as well as in considering the sorts of actions, structures and functions that impact upon the dissemination of works of Creative Writing. Certainly the idea that there is equality, throughout history and context, in the dissemination of Creative Writing is unhelpful, but so is any suggestion that final works, in whatever form, don't in some way compete against each other for the attention of readers/audiences. Of course, difficulties arise if Creative Writing is considered as *universally* socially orientated; or universally shared across time and space. A creative writer such Hermann Hesse speaks individually when he says 'the longer one works at it, the harder and more ambiguous the labour of language becomes'[10] even if the sentiment is expressed by other creative writers at other places and times. Likewise, to concentrate on construction to the complete marginalisation of constructed works belies good sense.

3.

A note on a relatively recent phenomenon: the world wide web (WWW).

If the 18th century introduced something new to how Creative Writing was received as a *thing* not an action, made, distributed and received, then the arrival in the late 20th Century of the WWW introduced something at very least equally significant. Much as the arrival of television and, later, free-standing domestic computer technologies, opened new avenues for the dissemination of final works of Creative Writing, the WWW also brought additional possibilities for the working and works of Creative Writing.

At first, it added to the range of possibilities in a complementary fashion, so that physical bookstores were complemented by 'virtual' bookstores, books available in one country were, relatively soon, available in another via the WWW, electronic games, disk-based reading, 'discussion lists'. The WWW arrived with complementary support but, when the technologies supporting it, and the hardware and software linked to it, advanced sufficiently then the WWW began to renovate the ways in which we could consider Creative Writing.

If, at first, the complementarity of the WWW seemed to suggest that it was a tool in support of the status quo, then its increasing reach, extended by greater bandwidth, by wireless (Wi-FI) communications, by faster, more robust and more cost-effective hardware and software, and by greater take-up throughout communities, made it plain that the WWW was not to take a support role but, rather, that it was taking a lead. It is now possible to engage in Creative Writing and disseminate final works without the involvement of a publisher, producer or bookstore – indeed, it is possible for anyone to create works and disseminate them without the involvement of an editor, designer, or printer. It is possible to produce works that incorporate not only written words but images and sound; that look something like traditional 'books' or that look nothing like them at all. It is possible – in fact, now very common – for a creative writer to gain an audience for their final works via the WWW and to extend that audience by 'word-of-mouth', that may involve 'words' but whose 'mouth' may more likely be the collection of social networking opportunities offered by the WWW.

Of course, again, all these observations are predicated on the notion of final works emerging from Creative Writing and being disseminated, more or less, in some fashion. The observation that the 'middle person or persons' between creative writer and reader was removed by the increasingly ubiquitous nature of the WWW deserves due recognition. But the WWW also introduced, and quickly extended, the idea of Creative Writing acts and actions revealed *in real time*. Meaning, that email initially, and personal, group, project websites later on, blogs, wikis and other tools and platforms, opened the possibility for the acts and actions of Creative Writing, even if not to be directly observed, to be considerably less detached from any artefact that was the result of Creative Writing. Additionally, with the notion of objectification challenged by WWW phenomena that produced 'virtual' rather than 'physical' artefacts, and with the WWW generally projecting ideals of immediacy and creativity (the number of creative activities and results of creative activities found on the web is large enough to be considered infinite) then the challenge to a cultural perspective that views Creative Writing as thing is strong.

Other technological advances have developed to add greater depth to this WWW challenge: on-demand publishing, which reduces the need, even if a physical 'book' is desired, for warehousing and, in combination with digital printing, makes construction and distribution of a book both financially and technically possible; digital media making, in general, which fuelled the growth of such paradigm shifting WWW entities as YouTube, where scripted and unscripted media challenged notions of traditional film distribution and media broadcasting; open-source design software that reduced the cost of creating hypertext or games orientated works and brought to the creative choices of creative writers new tools for incorporation of visual and aural materials; mobile phone technologies, which further spread the reach of the WWW as well as the modes and methods of Creative Writing dissemination, and added to the broader sense of connectivity between things 'in motion' (for example, the phone call 'on the move' being a very common activity by the last years of the 20th century).

Though it would assist the argument, it would be disingenuous to start suggesting here that the WWW returned us to the correct position of recognising Creative Writing as human acts and actions. Similarly, to suggest such a thing, while helpful in terms of grounding an argument for the complexity of the relationship between Creative Writing activities and artefacts, would be difficult to ground in that the WWW has also been a phenomenal promoter of commodity exchange and a mode for raising the extent of final works that might be offered as a thing, an object: 'Creative Writing'. Finally, it would be wrong to say that the WWW has increased equality of making and dissemination – this still relies on personal access, avenues for the acquisition of skills and for increasing the aptitude for applying them, technological infrastructure (both local and global), cultural preferences. The great website, linked to a blog, supported by a mainstream publisher's technical team, managed by a promotions company, designed by a professional designer – to take just one WWW example – has some advantages over the website in the hands of the creative writer without access to one or all of these things. And yet, the WWW very quickly introduced the *possibility* of widely available dissemination of the artefacts of Creative Writing and very quickly empowered a sense of Creative Writing as activity. It has been, in that way, a substantial challenge to the notions of Creative Writing brought about by a preference for final text as tradable artefact and for interaction to occur between creative writer and reader/audience primarily on the basis of a textual centrepiece.

Notes

1. Macoby, E.E. (1951) Television: its impact on school children. In *The Public Opinion Quarterly* 15(3), Autumn 1951, 435.
2. Cosgrove, J. and Morgan, M. (2000) The leisure activities of fifth grade pupils and their relationships to pupils' reading achievements. In *The Irish Journal of Education/Iris Eireannach an Oideachais* 01, 58–59.
3. Brewer, J. (1997) *The Pleasures of the Imagination: English Culture in the Eighteen Century*. London: Harper-Collins, p. 173.
4. Rose, M. (1994) *Authors and Owners: The Invention of Copyright*. Cambridge (MA): Harvard, p. 13.
5. Barthes, R. (1984) The death of the author. In S. Heath (trans. and ed.) *Image – Music – Text*. London: Fontana.
6. Knorr-Cetina, K. (1981) *The Manufacture of Knowledge: An Essay on the Constructivist and Contextual Nature of Science*. Oxford: Pergamon, p. 3.
7. Knorr-Cetina, K. (1981) *The Manufacture of Knowledge: An Essay on the Constructivist and Contextual Nature of Science*. Oxford: Pergamon, p. 12.
8. Knorr-Cetina, K. (1981) *The Manufacture of Knowledge: An Essay on the Constructivist and Contextual Nature of Science*. Oxford: Pergamon, p. 58.
9. Knorr-Cetina, K. (1981) *The Manufacture of Knowledge: An Essay on the Constructivist and Contextual Nature of Science*. Oxford: Pergamon, pp. 127–128.
10. Hesse, H. (1973) Events in the Engadine: 1953. In *Autobiographical Writings*. London: Picador, p. 220.

Chapter 6
There is Always a Direct Relationship Between Acts and Actions of Creative Writing and Disseminated Works?

1.

At what point does an act or action produce an artefact? By means of local definition, reiterating here that the definition of 'action' being used in this book is 'a collection of acts, sometimes joined by logic, intuition or fortuitous circumstance' and the definition of act is 'something done'. At what point, then, does either an act or an action produce an artefact, and is the relationship between works produced by Creative Writing and the acts and actions that are Creative Writing a direct relationship? To ensure clarity, the definition of 'direct' being used here is 'uninterrupted, without intervention, straightforward'. It will thus already be obvious that this statement only partially bears the weight of reality, and that it needs some considerable untangling in order to reveal where elements of truth might exist in it. Likewise, while touting the definitions being used – quite naturally, having offered them! – perhaps now also is the time to consider whether they need a little more untangling.

Anthropological investigations, because they explore the *behaviour* of humans, and it is behaviours (along with meanings, reasons, feelings, emotions, environments, physiological and psychological natures, understandings, knowledge) that we're considering when considering activities, offer some assistance here – with the specific interest on the relationship between artefacts and actions. Anthropologists undertaking research on how behaviours and artefacts relate in various cultures may therefore offer some directional assistance.

In an article published in *Man*, the journal of the Royal Anthropological Institute of Great Britain and Ireland, Michael O'Hanlon, exploring artefacts in relation to words and images in a Melanesian context, comments:

> [The] issue [...] of the nature of the relationship between words and images and the capacity (or otherwise) of words to express the

significance of images, is a topic that has long been of concern to interpreters of the rich artistic traditions of Melanesia. A major feature of Melanesian artistic traditions – remarked upon by all – is that the richness and evident significance of arts finds no counterpart in indigenous exegesis: people apparently have very little to say about artistic productions which are central to their economic, cultural and ritual lives.[1]

The author is looking to 'present ethnography to suggest we might want to break down the category of "verbalisation"' and that we might have concluded 'too swiftly that an absence of exegesis is the same thing as an absence of verbalisation'. If exegesis is absent, creating no artefactual, critical 'works' of its own, then the role of verbal communication, consciousness and tacitly shared knowledge becomes more obvious. With an interest in the creation and use of wigs worn during a particular festival he suggests that:

> For while the Highlanders in question do indeed offer very little *exegesis* of the significance of their wigs, they *do* talk about them, and while this may not account for all we might like to explain, it does have its own validity as being part of a wider local theory of significance [...].[2]

So the 'talk' is considered an aspect of creating and maintaining significance, and while this does not lead to more formalised critical explanation or analysis this is not talk without theoretical or critical validity; nor, O'Hanlon suggests, does the fact that it is not formalised mean that the 'verbalisation' undertaken has less importance within the making of, or the reception, of the artefacts. Further to this, the acts and actions of the creating, the making, are subject to their own broad set of principles, defined by the individuals, the groups, the culture and the circumstance so that while there may be personal activities going on these also find their way into 'verbalised' critical reception which may, in reverse, impact on the making itself. Thus:

> In the West we are familiar with the notion that art may have moral effects upon consumers; the Wahgi, in contrast, are interested in the way that art may reflect the moral conditions of its producers. Any difficulty in constructing a wig is likely to precipitate confessions from those present, who may reveal harboured grievances with each other.[3]

Thus, a moral and ethical dimension enters the making, as well as explanations of the making; a dimension that owes everything to how the makers are said to take responsibility for certain conditions of human interaction and to have a role in imbuing their art-making with appropriate morality. That this is located in confession (not of the Western religious kind but not far removed at all from the notion of the metaphysical, given that its intention is to improve 'harmony') relates to the sense in which the making involves more than mere physical action. This has relevance to how consideration of the creative always involves consideration of consciousness, and how consciousness works in such a way as to need to be considered in its entirety. Henri Bergson offers a useful analogical tool:

> A rapid gesture, made with one's eyes shut, will assume for consciousness the form of a purely qualitative sensation as long as there is no thought of the space traversed. In a word, there are two elements to be distinguished in motion, the space traversed and the act by which we traverse it, the successive positions and the synthesis of these positions. The first of these elements is a homogeneous quantity; the second has no reality except in consciousness [...]. On the one hand we attribute to the motion the divisibility of the space which it traverses, forgetting that it is quite possible to divide an *object* but not an *act*: and on the other hand we accustom ourselves to projecting this act itself into space, to applying it to the whole of the line which the moving body traverses, in a word, to solidifying it: as if this a localizing of *progress* in space did not amount to asserting that, even outside of consciousness, the past co-exists with the present![4]

Religious notions aside – and certainly these were something of what is behind Roland Barthes's opposition to the Author and declaration of the importance of the reader – religious notions aside, what Bergson observes here, and what O'Hanlon likewise realises in his anthropological study, is that present acts and actions and past acts and actions leave 'footprints' that might best be summed up as knowledge or understanding and that this knowledge or understanding, while sometimes represented by artefacts or objects can just as easily, and very readily, be represented by further acts and actions. This is a significant aspect of human exchange, but it is not without its socio-cultural, economic or political filters; it is not without intrusion of the holistic conditions under which individuals and groups live. The creative writer, then, while free within the confines of her or his room, at her or his desk, with her or his pencil or computer, is not entirely ever removed from such conditions and the directness of the association of acts and actions and the artefacts they produce –

pre-works/pre-working, complementary works/working, final works, and post-works/post-working – is determined by conditions of consciousness which can have both concrete and abstract manifestations. The thing, or action, that changes this is that of dissemination and O'Hanlon indicates this also in his study when he concludes:

> This is not simply in the sense that wigs prompt assessments – both within the limited community engaged in making the wig and amongst the spectators who comment on it when the wig finally 'comes outside' – but more importantly in the sense that people feel that they really do not know in any absolute sense what the true state of relations, within groups or between wig-wearers and their 'sources' actually is. All activities take place against a background of uncertain and contested knowledge.[5]

In contestation rests the parallel relationship between present and past, referred to by Bergson, and the difficulties of talking holistically about acts and actions that draw as much from personal dispositions as they do from cultural conditions. If Bergson and O'Hanlon point to one aspect of dissemination, which the WWW has most recently also highlighted, it is that reducing the distance between acts and actions and dissemination has a corresponding impact on a creative writer's consciousness, in which past and present at least partially dwell. And yet, even if focusing on the **event** of creation, the awareness that there is a **post-event** to any individual act asks us to consider how direct dissemination can ever accurately reveal acts and actions.

2.

Where this current analysis and Bergson's differs is in the ideals of duration and suggestions of indivisibility, because while Bergson is correct to emphasise mobility and freedom, in order to approach Creative Writing it has to be that the activity is seen to be producing something, some material evidence, some results of some kind. This can occur in a complementary way, one act of Creative Writing fluidly engaged with another, one work of Creative Writing emerging while others continue to be subject to writerly creation, or one emerging in one way while other emerges in another way (for example, the creative writer releasing a draft work and some working comments onto the WWW while publishing another work, a story say, in a print magazine) intersecting creative and critical (verbalised or exegetical) working and works. And Creative

Writing most often does work in this complementary way. But there is still a commonsense recognition that points of finality occur.

For this reason, acts and the actions to which they collectively contribute can be viewed as contributing to each **event** of Creative Writing – event meaning an occurrence, something taking place – while analysis of Creative Writing that occurs once an occurrence is recognised, concluded by release of a 'final' artefact, or superseded by evolution of an alternate occurrence, can be called **post-event**. The difference between creative writers and those who might analyse works completed by creative writers (ignoring, momentarily, that these works are subject a wide range of disseminational conditions and circumstances) is that the creative writer Creative Writing is combining event and post-event in the fluid way Bergson explores while the post-event critic, detached from the acts and actions of Creative Writing, is beginning with artefactual evidence, losing the connectivity on which Creative Writing occurs, regardless of whether explanation or exegesis exist to explore it. A direct relationship between acts and actions of Creative Writing and disseminated works could be said to occur – for some works, at least – for the creative writer but never for the purely post-event critic. Which places Barthes thoughts in striking relief, and suggests that the knowledge and understanding contained in the consciousness of the creative writer has a different aspect to that contained in the consciousness of the post event critic in other areas of investigation – such as that associated with the study of literature, drama, computer games, television.

The establishment of an *indirect* association is further engrained by intermediaries whose involvement is brought about by economic or political or social circumstances and is historically and culturally specific. So, for example:

(1)   publishing, producing, disseminating industries (in the case of the artefacts of Creative Writing, usually broadly part of the 'creative industries'), their scope and style and ability to influence. This can include conditions of public and private financing, the role of such industries in national and international economics and politics, the relationship between focus on product (perhaps most seen in commercially viable creative industries) and a focus on community or personal arts (perhaps most seen in publicly subsidised arts sectors). Historical notes here include such things as pre-industrial conditions of Creative Writing (in the West, the importance of the 18th century has been noted); similarly, non-mainstream exchanges

(for example, community exchange in writers' groups or the exchanges that have occurred during periods of patronage);

(2) the structure and importance of cultural groups. The implementing of more holistic than individualistic notions about disseminated works (for example, cultural conditions under which the acts and actions of a creative writer who produced a disseminated work is distanced by inclusion in structural conditions or functional approaches relating to the integrity or character of a established or emerging cultural group. Individual acts and actions are therefore distanced from group actions or group ideals);

(3) 'human' technologies, and the historical evolution of these. Seemingly superfluous to note technologies as 'human', given that the word 'technology', in one definition at least, refers to the very human 'science'. However, technologies can also refer to techniques for the manipulation of an environment and, in this sense, it is worth acknowledging that the technologies that have increased or decreased the distance between Creative Writing and the disseminated works emerging from Creative Writing have been introduced by humans to change or manipulate the human environment in which they live;

(4) the role of other individuals – for example, editors, publishers, designers, producers – in mediating the relationship between Creative Writing and the disseminated works of Creative Writing. In many cases, these individuals have been offering their own creative input, either less or more devolved from the activities creative writers, and their mediation incorporates both personal and public ideals, whether the taste and preferences of the individual or the policies of cultural or commercial entities.

The establishment or maintenance of an indirect relationship between the acts and actions of Creative Writing and disseminated works carries with its behavioural characteristics which reflect historio cultural contexts. It's useful to adopt that mode of thinking about History adopted by Annales historians[6] in which history can be considered in terms of the *longue durée* (long term historical structures), a favoured approach of Ferdinand Braudel and earlier Annalistes, cycles (patterns and reoccurrences) and episodes (immediate or short term incidents). In this way we can see moments when the acts and actions of Creative Writing have been more directly related to disseminated works (the impact of the WWW has been offered as one of these) and points where the relationship has been more distant (the introduction of copyright could be seen as one of those). We have seen cycles of creative writer behaviour – for example, the formation of salons, writers' groups or aesthetically defined associations – where within one circle or another actions and disseminated works have been relatively closely related. And we have seen the impact of the *longue durée* where the activities, the event, of Creative Writing, undertaken by a portion of the population, have been approached post-event by the analysis of others, separating the two human actions as if the disseminated artefactual evidence formed some kind of mortar between two bricks, rather than elements of fluid co-existence.

3.

Finally, some consideration of fortuitousness and irrationality. If it's acknowledged that 'the making of a piece of knowledge involves a series of decisions and negotiations'[7] then it needs to be equally acknowledged that any human exchange, in which a variety of understandings always occur, involves decisions and negotiations that do not involve rational negotiation or organised decision-making. The acts and actions that are Creative Writing are not *all* the result of rationality or of clearly refined psychologies. Similarly, the activities that constitute Creative Writing will have within their realm of influence social norms to which individual creative writers will, or will not, adhere more or less closely. The willingness to exchange, and reveal, the dimensions of the acts and actions of any particular creative writer can be influenced by the writer's belief system, by the feelings of whether their actions map onto social or, indeed, artistic norms, by the immediate personal circumstances of the creative writer's relationships or, quite simply, by the creative writer's ability or inability to capture (in memory as well in some physical way) the circumstances of creation.

A model of Creative Writing that made human agency the machine for the manufacture of creative products – whether those products were books, mobile phone texts, poems on the web, or anything else – would undermine the historically accurate observation that human beings have long shown the ability, in even the most extreme of controlled circumstances, to act with free will. Similarly, while intention might bear considerable weight, unintended results occur and these unintended results are as activating to the event of Creative Writing as those that are premeditated. The role of 'experience' has influence here because it could be said to confirm for the creative writer that certain actions will bring about certain results, only to show that unintentionality does not entirely disappear over time and thus raises questions then about the relationship between, say, technical writing skill and the ability to engage in Creative Writing. Alternatively, a tyro creative writer may produce remarkable final works, yet in their acts and actions reveal to themselves (and to anyone who might observe these actions) that much of the event here is not premeditated nor necessarily even understood and questions then arise as to the actual relationship between technical, aesthetic, communicative understanding and final works of Creative Writing. The social context of this might relate to forms of education, not necessarily any of them being formal. Christopher Lloyd suggests in relation to human agency that:

> Action is partly motivated and structured by the actor's experience of the world and knowledge of it, and particularly by the actor's perception of his or her interests, whether personal, institutional, or class interests. Action is therefore also structured by social context. Hence agency is never completely free but always constrained and enabled by its structural and ideological situation and by the experience of the actor.[8]

This further makes difficult any direct association between disseminated works and actual Creative Writing. Historically, this has made it more likely that the shorthand reference to certain final works, disseminated under the influences of cultural and/or economic conditions, would suffice as representation of event-focused understanding even if comments were borne out of post-event access to a limited range of artefactual evidence and therefore did not relate to actual practices or experiences.

Similarly, as it has been in the personal interests of individual creative writers, particularly in the context of patronage, commercial support, creating value, or simply in encouraging greater reader/audience belief in their abilities and thus allowing for wider dissemination of their ideas and thoughts, to suggest a direct relationship between actions and final results (much as Knorr-Cetina reports that scientists engage in 'opportunistic logic'[9]) then direct relationships between *actual* acts and actions and disseminated works has been weak. Add to that the considerable possibility that a creative writer's self-awareness, much as anyone else's, bears all the traits of how they view themselves as reference points and that this viewing, carrying only some portions of the true acts and actions that occur, along with a personal sense of ideal patterns, relevance and importance, is influenced by their capability and knowledgeability[10] and the distance between disseminated works and event of Creative Writing becomes considerable.

Notes

1. O'Hanlon, M. (1992) Unstable images and second skins: artefacts, exegesis and assessments in the New Guinea Highlands. In *Man*, New Series 27(3), 588.
2. O'Hanlon, M. (1992) Unstable images and second skins: artefacts, exegesis and assessments in the New Guinea Highlands. In *Man*, New Series 27(3), 590.
3. O'Hanlon, M. (1992) Unstable images and second skins: artefacts, exegesis and assessments in the New Guinea Highlands. In *Man*, New Series 27(3) 599.
4. Bergson, H. (2001) *Time and Freewill*. New York: Dover, p. 112.
5. O'Hanlon, M. (1992) Unstable images and second skins: artefacts, exegesis and assessments in the New Guinea Highlands. In *Man*, New Series 27(3), 605.
6. The Annales School of History, a French group of historians who favour social science methods in writing history and the study of social and cultural activities. 'No group of scholars has had a greater impact, or a more fertilizing effect, on the study of history in this century than the French historians of "the Annales school" – that is, to speak in more concrete terms, the historians whose base is in the sixth section of the *Ecole Pratique des Hautes Etudes* in Paris, whose books appear, in parallel series and steady flow, under the imprint of SEVPEN, Paris, and whose regular organ is that ample and ever-expanding periodical originally entitled *Annales d'histoire e'conomique et sociale* and now – that is, since 1947 – *Annales: e'conomies, societe's, civilisations*. French in origin, French in inspiration, these historians now form an international elite, held together by a distinct philosophy and a corporate loyalty and marked by a literary style which it is easy and sometimes tempting to parody.' Trevor-Roper, H. (1972) Fernand Braudel, the Annales, and the Mediterranean. *The Journal of Modern History* 44(4).
7. Knorr-Cetina, K. (1981) *The Manufacture of Knowledge: An Essay on the Constructivist and Contextual Nature of Knowledge*. Oxford: Pergamon, p. 40.
8. Lloyd, C. (1986) *Explanation in Social History*. Oxford: Blackwell, p. 281.
9. Knorr-Cetina, K. (1981) *The Manufacture of Knowledge: An Essay on the Constructivist and Contextual Nature of Science*. Oxford: Pergamon, p. 47.
10. ' "Action" refers to two components of conduct: "capability" and "knowledge-ability". By the first is meant that the agent "could have acted otherwise." The agent is therefore a being with individual and social *power*. "Knowledge-ability" refers to the practical consciousness of ordinary actors about their own society and the conditions of their own activities. It is not equitable with knowing consciously in the sense of "held in mind" but is, rather, the modes of tacit knowing about how to "go on" in social life. Neither is equitable with the ability to make decisions in the game-theoretic sense because it is less consciousness and less rational than that.' Lloyd, C. (1986) *Explanation in Social History*. Oxford: Blackwell, p. 309.

Chapter 7

The Activities that are Creative Writing Can Always be Grouped Under the Term 'Process'?

1.

Crack goes the pistol and off starts this entry.

Sometimes he has caught it just right; more often he has jumped the gun. On these occasions, if he is lucky, he runs only a dozen yards, looks around and jogs sheepishly back to the starting place. But too frequently he makes the entire circuit of the track under the impression that he is leading the field, and reaches the finish to find he has no following. The race must be run all over again ...

So runs an interview with one of the champion false starters of the writing profession – myself. Opening a leather-bound waste-basket which I fatuously refer to as my 'notebook', I pick out at random a small, triangular piece of wrapping paper with a cancelled stamp on one side. On the other is written:

Boopsie Dee was cute.

[...] There are hundreds of these hunches. Not all of them have to do with literature. Some are hunches about importing a troupe of Ouled Naïl dancers from Africa, about resuscitating football at Princeton [...]

These little flurries caused me no travail – they were opium eaters' illusions, vanishing with the smoke of the pipe, or you know what I mean. The pleasure of thinking about them was the exact equivalent of having accomplished them. It is the six-page, ten-page, thirty-page globs of paper that grieve me professionally, like unsuccessful oil shafts; they represent my false starts.[1]

F. Scott Fitzgerald writing about writing. There are an infinite number of similar examples: creative writers talking or writing about their experiences of Creative Writing. Edmund White, in a chapter entitled 'Writing Gay': '[...] Though I was a fairly bright student I had almost no skill as a writer. I wrote in a trance, almost unconsciously.'[2] Primo Levi, talking about writing on a computer: 'I'm still a neophyte: I still have to learn a lot of manoeuvres, but it would already cost me a great effort to go back to the typewriter, or, worse, ballpoint, scissors, and glue.'[3] Marianne Moore: 'It never occurred to me that what I wrote was something to define. I am governed by the pull of the sentence as the pull of a fabric is governed by gravity.'[4] Eudora Welty: 'My ideal way to write a short story is to write the whole first draft through in one sitting, then work as long as it takes on revision, and then the final version all in one, so that in the end the whole thing amounts to one long sustained effort.'[5]

There has been a concerted effort applied in this book, so far, to avoid using the word 'process' when referring to Creative Writing, in favour of talking about acts and actions and activities. 'Process', however, is quite often touted as an overarching term for a creative writer's activities and it is common to read about such a process, particularly in books about Creative Writing. There have even been entire books on Creative Writing with 'process' or 'processes' in their titles or in chapter titles[6]. Is it the right word to use for what Creative Writing involves, or it simply a word that has been adopted when a better word simply hasn't seemed available? Process certainly suggests a journey and etymologically owes something of its origins to exactly that notion: the sense of movement. However, there's something unwieldy here. Cecil Day Lewis, Poet Laureate of Great Britain from 1968–1972, remarked in a lecture given in 1956:

> We are compelled to speak of poetic process in metaphor. At this early stage, the poet has begun to build a house with only one small part of the blue-print available to him, or while he is still drawing the blue-print, or with many alternative blue-prints at his disposal. If he has to work in this hand-to-mouth way, it is because conception and form are far from inseparable, because a poem is an organic growth in which the theme only reveals itself through the growing pattern [...]. His activity during the initial stages of making a poem is equivalent to what Professor Young calls 'doubt' in scientific investigation: it is a rigorous questioning of data – data which include the poem's original subject, the secondary subject-matter which is attracted into the field of the poem out of the poet's wholelife-experience, and the formal patterns into which he is beginning to arrange it. The questioning is, for the poet as for the scientist, an arduous intellectual exertion.[7]

Here there's a sense in which Day Lewis is well aware of an experience – the experience of Creative Writing, and specifically of the writing of poetry – but is also aware that to talk of it as process doesn't quite grasp it. He reaches, thus, for 'blue-print', 'organic', 'growing'. Introduces 'stages'. Borrows 'doubt'. And concludes with reference to 'arranging' and 'questioning', rounding off with an almost celebratory note on the commonality of 'arduous intellectual exertion'.

Again Day Lewis seems to offer 'intellectual' as a slightly awkward shorthand for something to do with the operation of the mind, and the compulsion he notes to use metaphor to try and talk about what goes on in the writing of poetry is similarly significant here in that the word 'intellectual' seems to be equating with the concept of questioning. Henri Bergson would replace 'intellect' with *intelligence* and include a suggestion that *instinct* plays a substantial role, using both intelligence and instinct in his specific definitions. That is: Bergson associates intelligence with useful action, while what he calls 'instinct' is associated with life itself, intelligence being an adaptation.

'Instinct,' he writes, 'on the contrary, is molded on the very form of life. While intelligence treats everything mechanically, instinct proceeds, so to speak, organically.'[8] A combination of instinct and intellect, brought about by the application of intelligence, is a Bergsonian ideal, not least because the intellect on its own cannot approach life.

> [...] the intellect always behaves as if it were fascinated by the contemplation of inert matter. It is life looking outward, putting itself outside itself, adopting the way of organized nature in principle, in order to direct them in fact. Hence its bewilderment when it turns to the living and is confronted with organization. It does what it can, it resolves the organized into unorganized, for it cannot, without reversing its natural direction and twisting about on itself, think true continuity, real mobility, reciprocal penetration – in a word, that creative evolution which is life.[9]

Bergson sees intelligence as being 'turned' toward inert matter and instinct being 'turned' toward life. So they look in alternate directions, and in order to gain genuine knowledge he argues for what he defines as 'intuition'. For Bergson, intuition is instinct that is capable of reflecting, that is conscious of the self, is immediate, and has sympathy with what is around it. And it is telling that it is to art that Bergson refers in order to talk about this intuition:

That an effort of this kind is not impossible, is proved by the existence in many of an aesthetic facility along with normal perception. Our eye perceives the features of the living being, merely as assembled, not as mutually organized. The intention of life, the simple movement that runs through the lines, that binds them together and gives them significance, escapes it. The intention is just what the artist tries to regain, in placing himself back within the object by a kind of sympathy, in breaking down, by an effort of intuition, the barrier that space puts up between him and his model. It is true that this aesthetic intuition, like external perception, only attains the individual. But we can conceive an inquiry turned in the same direction as art, which would take life *in general* for its object, in following to the end the direction pointed out by external perception, prolongs the individual facts into general laws.[10]

Cecil Day Lewis's metaphoric reach for 'process' also reflects what Bergson is investigating here, and it is related to the communication that both Day Lewis and Bergson perceive between individual and wider world, between art and science, and between the internal world of the self (that is, our self-conscious sense of instinct and intelligence interacting in some way) and the external world of what we perceive and conceive. Thus, for Day Lewis Creative Writing, poetry writing, involves 'a kind of groping in the dark';[11] poetry can be 'a technique of knowledge'[12] and 'the poet is, above all, a maker'.[13] That this making, and this knowledge, includes some elements drawn from a instinct, and some drawn from intelligence, fluidly exchanging these, that it is not merely about internal self-consciousness but also about responding to the external world, and that it occurs by breaking down the barrier between the space of external and internal and between perception and memory, conception and action, suggests that the term 'process' is not entirely adequate to describe what occurs.

2.

'Process' is defined as 'progress, course',[14] 'a series of actions or steps towards achieving a particular end'[15] and a 'continuous series of actions meant to accomplish some result (the main modern sense)'.[16] In what ways might this have anything to do with Creative Writing? Certainly there are actions, more or less there is progress (depending on how we might define progress) and, broadly, the meaning attached to much of this relates to accomplishing 'a result'. However, it is doubtful the idea of a 'course' features as large as the idea of a process suggests, most definitely very little of this is 'continuous' and, even though one act may follow another, and be linked in any number of ways, it is difficult to imagine the concept of a 'series' adequately copes with the movements associated with conception, perception and memory that impact so greatly on Creative Writing.

It is important at this juncture not to confuse post-event analysis with event analysis; in effect, not to draw to our picture of how Creative Writing happens conceptual shorthand that undermines the fluidity of the interaction between instinct and intelligence (to use these terms as they are used by Bergson) and replaces this with a textual target, located as the conclusion, or promoted as both starting and end point.

To put it another way: if we begin with final results, material objects, and then think in reverse to their creation we quite naturally talk about results and progress. Why wouldn't we? We are, after all, *in sight* then of Creative Writing as material, objectified *thing*. How close we are to *actual* Creative Writing is questionable. But progress, a series, a course, that is leading somewhere, is strongly identified when a thing in existence is in front of us. Ted Hughes, another former Poet Laureate of Great Britain, and perhaps known by many as much for his life as his poetry, says of his well-known poem *The Thought-Fox:*

> If, at the time of writing this poem, I had found livelier words, words that could give me much more vividly its movements, the twitch and craning of its ears, the slight tremor of its hanging tongue and its breathing making little clouds, its teeth bared in the cold, the snow-crumbs dropping from its pads as it lifts each one in turn, if I could have got the words for all this, the fox would probably be even more real and alive to me now, than it is as I read the poem. Still, it is there as it is.[17]

'It is there as it is' for Hughes. But is it ended? Has the process been completed, for him? Perhaps, then, it wasn't a process at all.

We need to place textual or material evidence of Creative Writing within a continuum, identifying this as part of an ongoing exchange. This does not remove text from Creative Writing; nor does it suggest that creative writers don't have goals and, more pragmatically, it doesn't suggest that they are somehow devoid of the need to meet expectations (their own or those of others; for example, publishers, producers, directors, teachers, editors). But it does place textual evidence (which, as has been indicated, has tended to be only some evidence and only some evidence by only some creative writers) more accurately in the context of a dynamic. Toni Morrison, in a speech given when accepting the National Book

Foundation Medal for Distinguished Contribution to American Letters' comments for the occasion: 'I know now, more than I ever did (and I always on some level knew it), that I need that intimate, sustained surrender to the company of my own mind while it touches another's – which is reading [. . .] That I need to offer the fruits of my own imaginative intelligence to another without fear of anything more deadly than disdain – which is writing [. . .]'[18]

There are indications here of similar concepts to those of 'above all, a maker' offered by Day Lewis, and to Fitzgerald's 'hunches' and to Hughes's 'got the words for all this'. While Morrison is both reader and writer when writing she is offering up 'the fruits of my own imaginative intelligence', and in doing so she's entering an aesthetic and communicative mode which she recognises is distinctive. Human engagement with Creative Writing is multi-dimensional. Even if we could metaphorically consider this as a process or as processes, we could only accurately do so if we were to imagine these occurring across a three-dimensional plane, simultaneously, and this would fail to recognise that there are elements of singular linearity (not least in the life of the creative writer and in the holistic impact of cultural change, economic influence or individual and group politics on working and on works).

When considering writing generally it might be said that it is 'a visual medium of communication which circumvents or transcends certain limitations of speech'[19] and that it has five primary functions, as a mnemonic (it allows for a greater amount storage of information, knowledge, thoughts, than human memory can contain); to enable transmission over time and space (it allows for simple recording and transmitting over time and to different locations); as an instrument to create a codified record (as opposed to the more ephemeral nature of speech); as a *physical* art form involving language; and as a mode of normalisation and standardisation by which utterances are offered up to interpretation of meaning.[20] Even here, with the incorporation of memory and physicality (just to pick up two functions) the act of writing is not easily reduced to process. Add to this the adjective 'creative' (if, indeed, Creative Writing does involve an adjective and noun, which needs considering), with all that the imaginative and expressive entails and performs, and the notion of process becomes even less productive.

Creative Writing is not experiences alone, nor is Creative Writing simply its resultant texts. It is not often singular in motion, output or attitude. It is not always linear in direction, even if pieces are begun, have a journey of working, and are completed, in some sense or another. Its activities are not mechanical, even if they may draw on some of the mechanics of written language; its actions are not one dimensional, even if they work in an identifiable time and space. It involves fortuitousness, irrationality and emotionality, as well as planned action and rationality.

Notes

1. Fitzgerald, S. (1987) *Afternoon of an Author: A Selection of Uncollected Stories and Essays.* New York: Scribner, pp. 127–128.
2. White, E. (2004) *Arts and Letters.* San Francisco: Cleis, p. 5.
3. Levi, P. (1989) *Conversations. Primo Levi with Tullio Regge* (R. Rosethal, trans.). London: Tauris, p. 65.
4. Moore, M. (1961) Interviewed by D. Hall. *The Paris Review* 26, Summer-Fall 1961, 18.
5. Welty, E. (1972) Interviewed by L. Kuehl. In *The Paris Review* 55, Fall 1972, 23–24.
6. Some examples might include: Pearl Hogrefe's *The Process of Creative Writing*, New York: Harper, 1956 and a number of other editions; Wendy Bishop's *Working Words: The Process of Creative Writing*, New York: McGraw, 1991; Scott Barry Kaufman and James C. Kaufman, *The Psychology of Creative Writing*, New York: CUP, 2009, which contains a whole section entitled 'The Process'.
7. Day-Lewis, C. (1957) *The Poet's Way of Knowledge.* Cambridge: CUP, pp. 19–20.
8. Bergson, H. (1998) *Creative Evolution.* New York: Dover, p. 165.
9. Bergson, H. (1998) *Creative Evolution.* New York: Dover, p. 162.
10. Bergson, H. (1998) *Creative Evolution*, New York: Dover, p. 177.
11. Day-Lewis, C. (1957) *The Poet's Way of Knowledge*, Cambridge: CUP, p. 21.
12. Day-Lewis, C. (1957) *The Poet's Way of Knowledge*, Cambridge: CUP, p. 32.
13. Day-Lewis, C. (1957) *The Poet's Way of Knowledge*, Cambridge: CUP, p. 18.
14. *The Concise Oxford Dictionary*, London: OUP, 1976.
15. *The Compact Oxford Dictionary*, Oxford: OUP, 2009.
16. Online Etymology Dictionary, www.etymonline.com/index.php?term=process. Accessed 23.8.09. This dictionary notes that the modern sense of the word dates from 1627.
17. Hughes, T. (2008) *Poetry in the Making: A Handbook for Writing and Teaching.* London: Faber. First published 1968, p. 20.
18. Morrison, T. (2008). In C.C. Denard (ed.) *What Moves at the Margins: Selected Nonfiction.* Jackson: University of Mississippi, p. 190.
19. Coulmas, F. (1999) *The Blackwell Encyclopedia of Writing Systems.* Oxford: Blackwell, p. 158.
20. I have adapted these slightly from Florian Coulmas's *The Blackwell Encyclopedia of Writing Systems*, Oxford: Blackwell, 1999 – mostly to question whether codification equals quite the degree of social control suggested by Coulmas and, similarly, to question the elements of reification Coulmas suggests, from the point of view of Creative Writing as activities.

PART II

CONCERNING HUMAN ENGAGEMENT WITH CREATIVE WRITING

Creative Writing involves a set of activities, or process, that can be discovered by the investigation of disseminated works.

This proposition can be considered with reference to:

Chapter 8
All Works of Creative Writing Have Aesthetic Appeal?

1.

Not to overburden the 18th century with all things emerging in the name of modernity – and, earlier and later periods do need some clear consideration here – but in investigating aesthetic appeal, and beginning with the notion of a work of art, the 18th century does strongly feature. John Carey, in his book *What Good Are the Arts?*, says this:

> [...] the question 'What is a work of art? could not have been asked before the late 18th century, because until then no works of art existed. I do not mean that objects we now regard as works of art did not exist before that date. Of course they did. But they were not regarded as works of art in our sense. Most pre-industrial societies did not even have a word for art as an independent concept, and the term 'work of art' as we use it would have been baffling to all previous cultures, including the civilisations of Greece and Rome and of Western Europe in the medieval period. [...] in most previous societies, it seems, art was not produced by a special caste of people, equivalent to our 'artists', but was spread through the whole community [...]. The word 'aesthetics' was unknown until 1750, when Alexander Baumgarten coined it [...][1]

This has obvious connections with the earlier discussion of the commercial commodification of Creative Writing, copyright, ownership and the cultural commodification that draws on ideals that place particular value, for particular (often holistic, culturally determined and heritage-related) reasons in particular works and, thus, particular creative writers. If the idea of a work of art did not exist prior to the later 18th century, of course, then all this requires some contextual exploration.

We can find some assistance in a comparison of 'art for art's sake' versus 'art as utilitarian'. While the 18th century brought definite commodity changes it also was the location of a shift in which art became, increasingly, 'for art's sake' and the shift this brought about relates to whether works of art have intrinsic internal value, rather than value determined by their application. This then makes certain works more significant than others, in a way dissimilar to utilitarian analysis and with the intention of then assigning value and ownership according to that assessment of intrinsic worth. So when Jamie Andrews, in his role as Head of Modern Literary Manuscripts at the British Library, says 'compared to works of art [meaning visual art], the kind of money that we're talking about to acquire a literary archive is small fry'[2] he is articulating a clear contemporary definition of the intrinsic value of final works and evidence of working. And he is differentiating, even if this is only a connected intention, between the physical manifestation of 'a work of art' and the physical manifestation of a 'literary archive'. One is being valued as a work, one is being valued as evidence – there are connections between these two aspects, but the priorities informing the assessment are borne in this simple yet important statement.

Aesthetic appeal relates to a range of characteristics; 'properties commonly identified as aesthetic include beauty, elegance, grace, daintiness, sweetness of sound, balance, design, unity, harmony, expressiveness, depth, movement, texture and atmosphere'.[3] Degrees or dimensions of these, and connected characteristics, within final works produced by Creative Writing can be discovered, drawn out, responded to, even if no agreement is reached about whether a meaning can be applied to all, or parts, of such final works, or if there is debate as to the whether these characteristics are more or less strongly present, or if changes in cultural perception over time change how such characteristics are defined, or if one genre or another produced by Creative Writing gains, or loses, reader/audience support. However, works of Creative Writing that are not presented for critical examination – where do these stand in such an appeal to aesthetics? Certainly they would form part of a utilitarian consideration of Creative Writing; after all, they can be the frame on which final works are built or the origin of a style or form or structural condition that is developed and exchanged at the point of completion, or they can be the building blocks on which future works begin, or the post-textual representations of an ongoing set of actions relating to the creative writer's working. In all these cases a utilitarian approach to all the works emerging from Creative Writing would recognise the appeal of a work of Creative Writing on the basis of its application, its ability to accomplish the job that it was intended to accomplish.

However, a further element needs to be considered – that is, the affective response that a work of Creative Writing might induce: emotional states experienced by an audience or reader of a work of Creative Writing. It is hard to maintain that this is primarily utilitarian, though there could be an argument about the importance of certain kinds of emotionality as bonds within a societal context and, likewise, there might be a case to be made about the contribution affective responses make to communication between individuals and groups.[4] Overall, though, the idea of an affective component to Creative Writing and the works that emerge adds no greater clarity to the question of whether all works of Creative Writing have aesthetic appeal. Not all works of Creative writing produce affective responses, and not all produce affective responses of the same kind for different individuals or groups. So, while it might be true that works of Creative Writing can induce emotional states it is neither a challenge to certain works having aesthetic appeal nor confirmation that they do.

One element does arise from this however, that takes the investigation further back than the 18th century. Writing in *The Construction of Authorship*, Marlon B. Ross observes:

> [...] we could say that print gradually seduced the mind into thinking of mental experience in terms of individual possession. The medieval monk or scholar tended to conceptualize knowledge as that which was common to a culture [...] Authority, in this sense, is always proper, always an order of truth gleaned by some individuals perhaps better than others, but not possessed solely by any individual [...] Possessable authority, on the other hand, is a personal acquisition, which the individual mind has earned as a result of knowledge or experience created by the individual as a private being.[5]

If we view the aesthetic appeal of certain works of Creative Writing being heightened by the ability of others to acquire them – that is, having the authority of possession – then we can see how the creation of conditions in which works of Creative Writing can be owned by others and, in some ways, this ownership encompasses at least a tacit ownership of affective response.

If this is further enhanced by a selective mode of dissemination in which mostly final works of Creative Writing are privileged, and not all final works (for example, certain forms or styles or works by certain creative writers) then we have conditions in which aesthetic appeal is located only in internal characteristics but by the reference points established externally and made possible by modes of dissemination. Ross notes that we could 'trace the emergence of possessive authority as far back as the 12th century',[6] so this is no product solely of the commercial and cultural worlds emerging in the latter 18th century. And yet, any modern tension between utilitarianism and art for art's sake, which has relevance to a consideration of Creative Writing, undoubtedly owes something to the heightening of possessive authority which the developing ideal of a modern *market for culture*, initiated in the 18th century.

2.

John Updike once wrote that 'the itch to make marks on white paper is shared by writers and artists'.[7] He continued:

> Years before written words become pliant and expressive to their young user, creative magic can be grasped through pen and ink, brush and paint. The subtleties of form and color, the distinctions of texture, the balance of volume, the principles of perspective and composition – all these are good for a future writer to explore and will help him to visualize his scenes, even to construct his personalities and to shape the invisible contentions and branchings of plot.[8]

Of course, this from Updike who, though known by readers, and referenced by literary critics, almost entirely for his fiction, his novels, his poetry, spent 1954–1955 at the Ruskin School of Drawing and Fine Arts in Oxford, and who had desired to be cartoonist before he became a known creative writer. 'One can continue to cartoon, in a way, with words,' he remarked. 'For whatever crispness and animation my writing has, I give some credit to the cartoonist manqué.'[9] No hiding at all here of Updike's aesthetic sense.

> I always wanted to draw or write for a living [...] I have been able to support myself by and large with the more respectable forms – poetry, short stores, novels – but what journalism I have done has been useful. I would write ads for deodorants or labels for catsup bottles if I had to. The miracle of turning inklings into thoughts and thoughts into words and words into metal and print and ink never palls for me; the technical aspects of bookmaking, from type font to binding glue, interest me.[10]

At first glance, this would seem a comment in the same vein (that is, in relation to the attitude of the aesthete); but we see here a shift away from the authority of possession (object ownership; the reification of Creative Writing) so that Updike's could not rightly be called an 'art for art's sake' attitude, nor indeed is it purely utilitarian or driven by an entirely affective response. The physical activities of Creative Writing are his aspect of physiological and psychological exchange, his sense of connection; the representational nature of the book, not as object of Creative Writing, but as representative of 'turning', placing the appeal for Updike at the time of creation: 'thoughts into words', the making. His notions are artisanal, though like all of us he is, of course, drawn to the physically appealing. If aesthetic appeal involves both the appeal of the object and the appeal of the object's ability to initiate some affective response, even if it is not the only activity or object that might produce this response, then to consider writing as an almost universal mode of inscription is a good place to conclude this discussion.

For example, 'pictures of concrete objects stood at the beginning of Chinese writing. Linearization, reduction and conventionalization set in early. Hard surfaces like bone and shell favoured angular rather than rounded appearance of early characters, a design feature that was pre-served in brush writing. Since early characters were pictographic, their numbers proliferated with little conformity in their creation.'[11] Writing in general, whatever culture in which it emerged and at whatever point in history, has always included some element of aesthetic appeal. It is, as Marlon B. Ross and John Updike equally recognise in their considerations of print and of bookmaking, a thing that can create an attraction. Writing, that is, has physical form.

But when talking about Creative Writing something else exists. We have often devolved the physical attributes of the final works from the acts and actions that are Creative Writing (wrongly, but such has been the case). To consider aesthetic appeal in works of Creative Writing we often turn instead to those attributes associated with form, and even with genre, attributes such as elegance, grace, balance, design, unity, harmony. But this is rarely a universal assessment, nor does one or other final work have universal appeal: the tastes of the readers or audiences for Creative Writing determine the extent and type of much of this attraction. Of course, this also assumes preferential treatment for final works of Creative Writing. There is little doubt that many of the works of Creative Writing, those that are not final, and are often not disseminated, have highly varied levels of aesthetic appeal and that many of these would certainly not be considered by the creative writer as objects presented for aesthetic assessment, nor would their importance to Creative Writing be reduced were they to be purely utilitarian. Works of Creative Writing can, thus, have no aesthetic appeal, some aesthetic appeal (though it may not be universally shared), or a wide aesthetic appeal. While these objects or artefacts may form the basis of an exchange between maker and receiver of these works, they may represent only a small portion of the Creative

Writing that has been undertaken and their ability to bring about an affective response may, indeed, be less than the actions undertaken to produce them – meaning, that is, that while objects can solicit a human response so can movements, sounds, human expressions, moments of communication.

Notes

1. Carey, J. (2005) *What Good Are the Arts?* London: Faber, pp. 7–8.
2. Andrews, J. (2009) Interviewed by G. Harper, in C. Sullivan and G. Harper (eds) *Authors at Work: The Creative Environment.* Cambridge: Brewer, p. 76.
3. Cooper, D. (ed.) (1995) *A Companion to Aesthetics.* Oxford: Blackwell, p. 7.
4. Sigmund Freud suggested laughter, and circumstances associated with it, had the purpose of offering 'psychic release', channelling energy which could otherwise have resulted in violent behaviour. This kind of function, linked to a wider range of emotional responses, could be applied to the works of Creative Writing. Whether it would relate to all works, however, is highly unlikely.
5. Ross, M.B. (1994) Authority and authenticity: scribbling authors and the genius of print in the eighteenth century. In M. Woodmansee and P. Jaszi (eds) *The Construction of Authorship: Textual Appropriation in Law and Literature.* Durham (NC): Duke, p. 235.
6. Ross, M.B. (1994) Authority and authenticity: scribbling authors and the genius of print in the eighteenth century. In M. Woodmansee and P. Jaszi (eds) *The Construction of Authorship: Textual Appropriation in Law and Literature.* Durham (NC): Duke, p. 236.
7. Updike, J. (2007) Writers and artists. In D. Friedman *The Writer's Brush: Paintings, Drawings and Sculpture by Writers.* Minneapolis: Mid-List, p. 429.
8. Updike, J. (2007) Writers and artists. In D. Friedman *The Writer's Brush: Paintings, Drawings and Sculpture by Writers.* Minneapolis: Mid-List, p. 430.
9. Updike, J. in F. Storrs (2009) Exhibit B: John Updike's doodles. *Boston Magazine*, March 2009.
10. Updike, J. (1968) Interviewed by C.T. Samuels. *The Paris Review* 45, Winter 1968, 12.
11. Coulmas, F. (1999) *The Blackwell Encyclopedia of Writing Systems.* Oxford: Blackwell, p. 79.

Chapter 9

All Works of Creative Writing Clearly Communicate?

1.

The notion of clear communication in works of Creative Writing raises the question of what kind of communication Creative Writing is in the first place. Obviously, it is not the same kind of communication as, say, non-written communication. Or is that not so obvious? That is, does Creative Writing share something in common with communication in the visual arts or performance arts: for example, in painting, classical or popular music, drawing, photography, drama? If so, on what basis might this constitute communication and what kind of communication might this be?

Obviously Creative Writing communication shares much with communication in forms of writing? Or is that, also, not so obvious? That is, does Creative Writing share relatively little in common with professional writing; for example, with what is often, in some academic systems, discussed in the realm of rhetoric; with technical writing, the writing of reports, informational website writing, the composition of legal documents and briefs, the writing of advertising and marketing documents?

The problem or, perhaps better said, the answer to these questions lies in the concept of the creative. Rob Pope, in his book *Creativity: Theory, History, Practice*, notes the emergence of the word 'creative' as being as recent as 1875.[1] Decidedly, then, Creative Writing could not precede that date by very much then. However, of course it did, but under different labels. D.G. Myers locates some movement between *doing* and *critically examining* poetry also in the period around the late 1870s, with a reference to the poet Edward Rowland Sill who 'would become one of the first poets to teach college English, serving from 1874 to 1882 as a professor at the University of California.'[2] No particular assistance with the concept of creativity but an interesting chronological juxtaposition in this discussion, given that this represents the nascent sense of formal Creative Writing classes on campus. Bergson's *Creative Evolution* was first published in

English 1911, though it had appeared as *L'Evolution créatrice* in 1907. Clearly, in translation, the word creative had by the early 20th century found a home. All seemingly well, then. Or not ...

David Bohm, in *On Creativity* published in 1998, declares: 'creativity is, in my view, something that it is impossible to define in words.'[3] And yet, though Bohm is wary of attempting a definition 'in words' he does nevertheless offer:

> [...] originality and creativity begin to emerge, not as something that is the result of an effort to achieve a planned and formulated goal, but rather as a by-product of a mind that is coming to a more nearly normal order of operation. And this is the only way in which originality and creativity can possibly arise, since any effort to reach them through some planned series of actions or exercises is a denial of the very nature of what one hopes to achieve. For this reason, originality and creativity can develop only if they are the essential force behind the very first step.[4]

So Bohm brings together creativity and originality, and suggests neither results from plans or formulations of goals, or from a 'planned series actions or exercises'. Rather, that both originality and creativity are a 'by-product'. To apply this to the defining of *Creative* Writing, then, we'd need to suggest that the creative is a consequence or a side-effect, that it is a derivative. This would be disempowering, if not quite simply illogical, suggesting that somehow the activity of writing, generally, becomes writing, creatively, through a lack of attention to plans.

Not to advocate, or not advocate, planning in the realm of Creative Writing; but, Bohm's description seems to be more about the importance of the fortuitous, which is not irrelevant but is not a definition. Similarly, we might wonder what it is to alter from a discussion of *creative* to a discussion of *creativity*. *Creative* as description of something occurring, something adjectival – that is something specifying, qualifying – where as *creativity* carries the weight of a definition of ability. The terms, though quite obviously related, are thus entirely different in perspective. Interestingly, the word *creativeness*, which is also a noun form relating to create or creation, is less well-known, though its definition relates to a quality, a characteristic, a trait.

Showing all the features that date it, but nevertheless perceptive, the following by Eva Mary Grew, part of an article entitled 'The Creative Faculty' published in the journal *Music and Letters* in 1946, seems to grasp something of the circumstance that it is investigating:

Thus the artist of creative genius is compelled to utter himself. Indifferent to social success or the taste of possible patrons [...] The knowledge and feeling that are the substance of his art are of the kind that irresistibly demand outlet and expression. Whether he creates hastily for bread or leisurely for love, his labours are in this respect like the operations of nature, which cannot be arrested [...] The technical equipment of these men is again like that of nature: it is habit become second nature, like the habit of speech or that of balancing the body upon the feet. It holds awareness of the proportions and harmonies inherent in all natural phenomena – in the universe itself. Technique is mental as well as material. It is of the mind as well as of the hand; and in both directions it is, to a certain extent, self-animating and self-conditioning, though it can never be mistaken for the art itself.[5]

The creative in this description is about awareness, about having a relationship with the natural in having a similar temporal and spatial approach, in general ways of working; and that this is not about externally imposed notions (such as whether this creative activity is undertaken for personal satisfaction, for employment, or for a combination of both) but about the self and, importantly, about 'the mind as well as the hand'.

Such a definition might fall foul of close inspection if it was based in objects. But if we correctly view Creative Writing as acts and actions, then the adjectival recognition of something specific begins to make sense. And that, as Eva Mary Grew observes, involves ways of thinking as well as ways of acting. We can consider then if Creative Writing involves the same kind of clarity that we might expect from other forms of writing or, indeed, if in being creative (which is its specifying and qualifying feature) it owes something to alternative modes of action and communication which are shared, in some way, with other creative forms. Oliver L. Reiser, whose philosophy extended well beyond that connected with the creative, offers something of assistance here, in questioning a duality of thought:

If, then, we grant that substance and action, like quantity and quality, are the logical limiting notions of an ontological essence which, in reality, is both (i.e. substance-action or a quantity of quality), we must next ask ourselves, what is the analytical unit out of which the creative and evolving universe is to be constructed?[6]

Reiser is considering ontology (that is, the nature of being) and our behaviour in attempting to engage with this nature of being. But if we consider Creative – Writing (described, momentarily, in this split way) as a duality, we can recognise something of the problem that he is talking about, albeit more widely. It is the considering of Creative Writing not as something specific, in its entirely, but falsely as a creative version of writing that confuses our thinking. Creative Writing is not two sets of behaviours, it is one set, and whatever artefactual evidence emerges from it thus needs to be considered, in that sense, monistically not dualistically. Then we can address the question of what clarity might mean in that instance, not least because such a sense of dynamic synthesis, bringing together activities and artefacts, is supported already by how Creative Writing actually occurs.

2.

'The function of art,' says Ranjan Ghosh, 'is not merely to communicate certain unalterable messages – a task that is well accomplished by even non-artistic devices':

> It may be the case that some works of art are used for the limited purpose of making social, political and religious propaganda. Communicability in such instances is extra-artistic and by no means an essential feature of art. Art does not deal with mere information. It aims at transforming and uplifting the sensibility.[7]

Here Ghosh places, if not in opposition at least at different places on a spectrum, information sharing and the ability to perceive and feel (that is, sensibility). He may or may not be right to separate these ideals. After all, both could be incorporated into a concept of awareness, with each bringing to awareness a component, cognitive, emotive, psychological, behavioural, for example. And yet, his aim is as significant as it is simple because what Ghosh is looking to oppose is any 'theory of communication' that claims 'that art communicates ideas and feelings without identifying the distinctive *way* in which this may happen.'[8] In looking for something distinctive, therefore, Ghosh situates his analysis in terms of a binary – that is, art versus not-art – and in doing so he quite naturally seeks out difference, locating this in information distinguished from sensibility. This is certainly grasping at something, but it's not quite firmly grasped.

In the case of Creative Writing, a relationship with a discussion of art and communication needs to be undertaken with the monistic context in mind. Adopting Ghosh's approach, if this were not the case it would be simple enough to locate the elements of art in 'creative' (and thus, sensibility would live here) and the elements of communication in 'writing' (and this would be the site of information). But this binary entity is not what Creative Writing is; rather, Creative Writing is an entirety, a whole.

With this in mind, Creative Writing as art incorporates its identity as inscription and its identity as physical as well as mental communication. The notion of clear communication in Creative Writing, therefore, incorporates communication of sensibility as well as information. And, naturally, noting that all works of Creative Writing are not final works or works intended for release to a readership or audience, and that works of Creative Writing are only a small portion of Creative Writing itself.

Those things said, works of Creative Writing have appearances – not simply in terms of the physical appearance of writing as notion but in terms of the arrange arrangement of words on page or screen, in stone, on canvas, in the spoken words of character, avatar, or pop singer, to name just a few instances. Those appearances will more, or less, draw attention; and, further, attention may be afforded certain things said, things said in certain ways, ideas conveyed, images evoked. This constitution of appearance will have an impact on how clear the communication might be. So that one appearance or another of a work of Creative Writing, depending on readership or audience, might combine differing levels of clarity, whether that clarity relates to information and/or sensibility.

Creative Writing may display, more or less so, clarity in belief or bias. It may involve, in effect, a combination of empathic and phatic communication; that is, communication that is attempted with entirely focal intent on ideas or issues that ideals, or communication that attempts to establish a relationship, without necessarily grounding this in an agreement of type or association or vision. Thus its 'clarity' may alter, shift around, regardless of the strength of purpose. Creative Writing may motivate a reader or audience to read or engage further, perhaps by appealing to a sense of self-actualisation or self-esteem, or by an appeal to belonging, or by the stimulation of the senses. Or it may not motivate at all, especially via such things as offering security or appealing to the spiritual. It may, indeed, do both or neither.

Works of Creative Writing may appear to be acutely aware of inter-personal communication, locating their communication in a situation or context, or in a set of codes, that relate to the community experiencing the works of Creative Writing. So, for example, a national arena, a con-temporary context, an appeal to codes relating to sexuality or gender, the codified context of a consumer group (say, for example, the consumers of popular music), or the interpersonal communicative modes adopted by certain age groups. There may, or may not, be consensus on the information or:

Works of Creative Writing are, by nature, carriers of the acts and actions with which creative writers undertaking Creative Writing have engaged. But they are not Creative Writing and, therefore, the extent to which they are not distorted by conveyance or by the barriers of transferring from one site of activity (Creative Writing) to another (receiving works) is varied. The clarity perceived in works of Creative Writing is also defined by convention so that should one form of delivery, one mode of representation, one physical object, be seen to incorporate Creative Writing more than another (for example, the physical shape and design of a book be more conventionally associated with the form of the novel than any other object) then clarity of communication may also be determined by how close a particular work of Creative Writing references this convention. The same can be said in terms of commercial or cultural value: both have notable effects on clarity as both impact on notions of need and on the ways in which creative writers and readers/audiences perceive the cultural environment.

Considered, as it should be, in accordance with its monistic nature, all works of Creative Writing cannot possibly clearly communicate – to all people, at all times, in all circumstances. And yet, some will communicate, more or less clearly, in abundant and diverse ways, some associated with what many have come to emphasise in the forms of communication noted in art and some associated with the forms of communications noted in writing. The reality being, of course, that works of Creative Writing – particularly those which are offered as documents of exchange between creative writer and reader or audience – these works are indivisibly vessels of information and sensibility.

Notes

1. Pope, R. (2005) *Creativity: Theory, History, Practice*. London: Routledge.
2. Myers, D.G. (1996) *The Elephants Teach: Creative Writing Since 1880*. New Jersey: Prentice Hall, p. 15.
3. Bohm, D. (1998) *On Creativity*, London: Routledge, p. 1.
4. Bohm, D. (1998) *On Creativity*, London: Routledge, p. 26.
5. Grew, E.M. (1946) The creative faculty. *Music and Letters* 27(2), April 1946, 102–103.
6. Reiser, O.L. (1924) A monism of creative behaviour. *The Journalism of Philosophy* 21(18), 28 August 1924, 480.

7. Ghosh, R.K. (1987) Artistic communication and symbol: some philosophical reflections. *British Journal of Aesthetics* 27(4), Autumn 1987, 324.

8. Ghosh, R.K. (1987) Artistic communication and symbol: some philosophical reflections. *British Journal of Aesthetics* 27(4), Autumn 1987, 319.

Chapter 10
Intentions in Creative Writing are Always Met?

1.

The acts and actions of Creative Writing can be associated as much with intention as they can with fortuitousness (that is, with the unintended or unpredictable). This seemingly unassuming statement nevertheless bears fruit when it is approached to determine the nature and extent of the rapport between intentionality and Creative Writing. Approaching this statement another way, and with an eye to avenues of education: if Creative Writing does *not* involve some element of intention being met then how is it that educationalists claim to be able to teach it (to varying extents and with varying claims of success)? However, if it can be taught, or learnt, then why do so many who undertake it complain of their inability to match intention and action, action and result?

It needs little further unfolding to reveal the extent of the seeming devolution of intention, action and result. For example, Faulkner, lamenting: 'it ran dry after about two days, I was miserable, kept at it, the stuff was no good, I would destroy it every night and still try again tomorrow, very bad two weeks [...].'[1] And Marge Piercy, revealing: 'my urge to write fiction comes from the same part of my psyche that cannot resist eavesdropping on strangers' conversations in airports, in restaurants, in the supermarket.'[2] And E.L. Doctorow, recalling origins:

> An earlier novel, *The Book of Daniel*, was conceived during a period of enormous national torment, the late '60s, with the war in Vietnam raging and the divisions among our generations deeper than any time since the Civil War. Another private excitement of the writer is his sudden awareness of the historically systematic unfairness of things. This particular resolution into pain of an intellectual commonplace can hardly be suggested by the word excitement. The writer writes from an almost biblical anger, which is not much different from despair. It is a dire, driven state of mind that professes and, at the same time, refuses to accept the truth that, as individuals, humans are

pitiful, and as groups, inhuman. *The Book of Daniel*, a novel reflecting on an espionage conspiracy trial in the '50s, and its aftermath in the '60s, was composed out of that unassuageable feeling.[3]

It is relevant, but a larger question than encompassed here, to consider what generally constitutes an 'intention'. Intention can include desire and belief, because while it incorporates the sense of being related to *action*, it also includes the sense of relating to an *aim* or to *aims*. With aims and actions being integral to intention, it then resolves to relate to explanation, referring what is intended (acts and actions) to what is desired, required, believed, and to what is done.

Logically, therefore, the intentions of an individual or group can be mapped well onto their beliefs and desires, and the actions that result can be considered before, during, and after they are undertaken according to the map that is developed. And yet, intention expressed does not always result in intention realised. To take one instance: a creative writer may say 'I am visiting New York next week, Hell's Kitchen mostly, to do some research for an historical novel about the European discovery of Manhattan Island'. Ultimately, while acting on this intention, the writer may go on to produce, alternatively, a short story and two poems drawing on discoveries about the crew of Henry Hudson's yacht the *Halve Maen*, connected with sightings of Manhattan but not ultimately about Manhattan. A novel concerned directly with the history of Manhattan Island might never emerge; but the intention to produce one may result, further, not only in more short stories set on-board Hudson's ship (which, incidentally, transmogrifies into a space craft and the USA into a planet not unlike Jupiter in size and distance and colouring) but also in the writing of a novel about the contemporary town of Halfmoon in Saratoga County, New York, where the central character, Ethan Kale, is born, grows to young adulthood, discovers his Irish roots, ruins his chances with Grace Summers over some crack about her and Hank Magarelli and, three times divorced and married to Grace's one-time best friend Abbie, ends up President of the Technisoft Corp.

The situation, above, that produced an aim and an action was connected with reasoning which weighed up, in some fashion, alternative decisions on what should be done. It might have been possible, for example, to explore writing a novel about the history of Manhattan by spending a week as a guest at the New York Stock Exchange, or by reading extensively about the Triangle Shirtwaist Factory fire or by looking at the global business of advertising and the role of Madison Avenue in supporting it. Of course, the strength of intention, argued internally as well as revealed externally, creates reason which, when faced with alternatives, favours a visit to Manhattan, Hell's Kitchen mostly, above the alternatives, which then fall by the way.

But what if, on the journey to Manhattan, the creative writer – travelling down from his hometown of Trigger, a fine town in upstate New York, mostly devoted to the manufacture of finely tufted mattresses and to the memory of Colonel Mitchell, who saved the town from the flood of '48 and recovered the founding daughters from the raging torrent – the creative writer has just made the turn onto I-81 and should, according to intention, continue down the 81 for another one hundred and thirty one miles until he reaches the I-84 when, on seeing a sign for Thomson's Bakery and favouring a creamed bun at lunchtime, he decides to pull off and head instead into the city of Binghamton. There, unbeknown to him, Arlene Ardella Thomson, whippet like doyenne of the Thomson family, as green of eye as she is slender of curve, has just baked a batch of the best Blueberry Cream Cheese Buns she has ever baked, and placed them proudly on her wire rack in the window.

There is no chance now that this creative writer will continue to Manhattan, seated so comfortably as he is outside Thomson's, with a bun in his hand and a coffee nearby. And, therefore, there is no chance he will directly produce any works related to the visit to Manhattan, however indirectly they may have been related. At least, he will not produce any works that are *physically* connected to the original intention. Of course he may, pondering on intentions that are not met, undertake some Creative Writing that picks up on the theme of a loss of direction or that, in investigating the subject of great bakeries, explores the ingredients leading to success and failure and offers a recipe for life. Of course, this is all becoming trite! But the meaning is sound: did the abandonment of intention mean that the intention was not real, was not truthful, or merely that it was not strong enough? Alternatively, could we view the decision to change the journey, and ultimately conclude it, in Binghamton as a new intention which therefore, containing more pressing desires and more firm beliefs, overcame the previous intention and created a new set of acts and actions?

Acts and actions are not, naturally, irrevocable and it is not necessarily a sign of a lack of commitment, or of a weakness of mind generally, to change acts and actions. This makes Doctorow's declaration of 'that unassuageable feeling' an interesting declaration because there is a plain indication here of the writer's self-referential landscape, so that Doctorow joins the strength of his belief with the strength of his intention and, as the language he uses indicates, there's little encouragement to be had here for divergence from thematic aims or subject. This suggests an almost immovable moral imperative, with the comment that 'the writer writes from an almost biblical anger, which is not much different from despair' leaving little doubt that Doctorow associates the desire in his intentions with the *desirable*. Such is the broad context of his personal reasoning.

Reasoning in Doctorow's case will not be the same as reasoning in Piercy's or reasoning in Faulkner's. More so, a creative writer's post-event analysis of intention will not only reveal much of their own sense of their acts and actions but will also be influenced by how the creative writer sees themselves and by their own deliberations, after the events have been undertaken. Likewise, a creative writer's post-event analysis of their intentions will, frequently, reflect degrees of social exchange and social interaction with which they are then engaged, and how they wish to engage with these. Alternatively, intentions during the event of Creative Writing (that is, consideration at the point of acts and actions), while possible, will reveal the limitations that immediacy entails, with tendencies, abilities and competencies only as discernible as their close performance might suggest.

How far the statements and recollections of Faulkner, Piercy and Doctorow qualify as 'intentions' is open to more consideration; after all, Faulkner's comments are perhaps intentions in the broadest sense only, revealing his ideal situation of satisfactorily writing the work at hand; Piercy talks about an 'urge', which may perhaps be substituted for 'desire', but may just as logically refer to a 'drive', which can be an action but may be not as related to the operations of belief or reasoning as is intention; and Doctorow's comments certainly reveal a strong and clear attitude of mind but don't necessarily unify that particular attitude with a set of Creative Writing acts.

To return, momentarily, to the question of the learning and teaching of Creative Writing. Auden fearful of the impact teaching in a college or university environment would have on the reasoning undertaken by a creative writer, offers:

> [...] artists should agree not to have anything to do with con-
> temporary literature. If they take academic positions they should do
> academic work, and the further they get away from the kind of thing
> that directly affects their writing, the better.[4]

The further, that is, from the interruption of extrinsic influences which may, as intimated by Auden, result in a mismatch of intention and action and, more obviously, intercede in creative activities by inserting super-fluous modes of acting or thinking. Of course, Auden was generally sceptical about the intersection of Creative Writing and the world, at least in that sense, commenting that 'so many people have jobs they don't like at all. I haven't, and I'm grateful for that.'[5]

Auden's comments alert us to the consideration of intention and causation – they may be practical connection between some acts and intentions, and not others, some creative writers (and not others) may have dispositions which encourage them to hold more tightly to their own laws of composition, while others would find even the notion of a 'law' an affront; and reasoning may be presented as good or bad, efficient or inefficient, well undertaken or poorly actualised, depending on where the creative writer believes themselves to be in the actions they are undertaken, depending on how their results are relating to their perceived goals, and depending on how external factors are influencing their perspective.

Cause and effect, states of mind (both conscious and unconscious), perceived goals, experiential evidence, prior knowledge, learning and discovery during the activities of Creative Writing, beliefs, personal propositions: these all no doubt establish points of communication, some drawn from intention (whether longer term reasoning and planning, or short term) and some occurring unexpectedly. The role of consciousness and the unconscious in forming intentions begs the question of how simply one state might be devolved from the other. Memory plays a role; and the movement between event and post-event analysis, pre-working, complementary working and post-working all determine how intention evolves, and adjusts. Combine this with the representational qualities of the acts and actions of others and of the material objects, and systems of signs and symbols we daily encounter, and intention becomes a personal and public matrix, containing both intrinsic and extrinsic elements.

2.

Plainly, then, intentions in Creative Writing can always be met if the way in which intention is defined incorporates a number of important qualifying elements. If it doesn't, intentions are only occasionally fully met, and only very rarely would we talk in terms of purely intention-fuelled Creative Writing. However, intention incorporating the following elements is readily observable and frequently a component of Creative Writing: that is, incorporating the possibility of unexpected change, adjustment of direction according immediate circumstance, the impact of extrinsic factors (often meaning the representational qualities of objects or actions brought about by others), the possibility of losing the will to continue (that is, the replacement of one intention with a stronger intention; or, as a sub-set of this, the replacement of one desire with a stronger desire), the possibility of complementary effects so that one intention might generate more effects than had been envisaged, the vast majority of these entirely unintentional.

Returning to Faulkner's 'very bad weeks', his goal could broadly be expressed as 'completing the work at hand' and certainly Faulkner seems to suffer greatly when he feels he is not meeting that intention. He writes, barely a month after his earlier letter: 'Am so near the end of the big one that I am frightened, that lightning might strike me before I can finish it. It is either nothing and I am blind in my dotage, or it is the best of my time.'[6] Bruce Aune would no doubt describe Faulkner's lamenting as a propensity 'to premiss things under indefinitely conceived conditions'.[7] That is, Aune argues that beliefs and intentions are best understood as 'incompletely specified conditional properties,'[8] suggesting that as the concepts of belief and intention are 'nontechnical locutions' they must not be defined in a determinist fashion or they will fail to 'describe the believing and intending' we *actually* experience. Faulkner's intentions, while discernible, are incomplete – much as, not inconsequentially, is the Creative Writing he is undertaking at the time of letters. Aune's argument contrasts a little with that of one of his fellow philosophers, Bertram Morris, expressed half a century earlier. Says Morris:

> In the keen perceptual fullness achieved both in creation and appreciation is the verification of art as communication. Continuity is thus established between the physical and the social, and culture is safeguarded by reason of the physical becoming germane to experience. In this accomplishment imagination is satisfied as a value made concrete and shareable by all who have the requisite patience and psychological disposition. In this accomplishment a purpose is expressed in a sensuous medium.[9]

Certainly we can acknowledge the role of disposition, of sensibility, of the physical and of the psychological in the formation of intention. Whether imagination can be made concrete or culture safeguarded is questionable. However, what's clear even in this assessment is that continuity defines the way in which intention occurs in the arts, and in this case in Creative Writing specifically, and that this continuity involves thought and action, desire and belief, and while intentions may not always be met they form a part of the network of intended and unintended activities and results that are Creative Writing.

Notes

1. Faulkner, W. (1977) Letter of Joan Williams, Friday night 3 July 1953. In J. Blotner (ed.) *Selected Letters of William Faulkner*. New York: Random House, p. 350.
2. Piercy, M. (2001) Life of prose and poetry: an inspiring combination. In J. Darnton, *Writers on Writing: Collected Essays from The New York Times*, intro. New York: Holt, pp. 180–181.
3. Doctorow, E.L. (2003) From will-o-the-wisp to full-blown novel. In Marie Arana (ed.) *The Writing Life: Writers on How they Think and Work*. New York: Public Affairs, p. 208.
4. Auden, W.H. (1974) Interviewed by M. Newman. *The Paris Review* 57, Spring 1974, 7.
5. Auden, W.H. (1974) Interviewed by M. Newman. *The Paris Review* 57, Spring 1974, 37.
6. Faulkner W. (1977) Letter of Joan Williams, Friday night 3 July 1953. In J. Blotner (ed.) *Selected Letters of William Faulkner*. New York: Random House, p. 352.
7. Aune, B. (1990) Action, inference, belief and intention in philosophical perspectives. *Action Theory and Philosophy of Mind* 4, 268.
8. Aune, B. (1990) Action, inference, belief and intention in philosophical perspectives. *Action Theory and Philosophy of Mind* 4, 268.
9. Morris, B. (1940) Intention and fulfilment. *Art, Philosophy and Phenomenological Research* 1(2), Dec 1940, 153.

Chapter 11
Creative Writing is Solely an Act or Range of Acts?

1.

Acts, of course, are defined in this discussion as 'something done' and actions are constituted of a collection of acts. Naturally, were the question above a statement that Creative Writing consists solely of acts it would be very difficult to maintain (and, indeed, illogical), given the existence of works produced by activities of Creative Writing. However, as much has been made here of the need to consider Creative Writing as a human activity, the statement does raise questions about the nature of acts of Creative Writing, about how such acts are associated and how we can determine, examine, consider a range of Creative Writing acts and actions which are independent from, partially dependent on, or entirely dependent on, each other. As Henri Bergson points out, it is quite possible to divide an *object*, but not an *act*. And, indeed, Creative Writing has so far be presented as indivisible and this discussion has emphasised the ways in which considering it this way gets closest to how we might come to understand it.

Creative Writing as acts and actions, grouped generically as activities, produces physical evidence of various kinds, as well as evidence observable and recordable as it emerges in and around the acts and actions that constitute Creative Writing. The evidence in this case is in the realm of the doing, behaviour, performing, movements and perhaps most provocatively, it could also be said to be in the realm of function.

By suggesting that the acts and actions of Creative Writing can be considered in terms of their function, there's equally a suggestion that those acts and actions that are unplanned, fortuitous, seemingly unsystematic (and more on this in a moment) are elements of the way in which Creative Writing occurs. That is, in acknowledging that all elements of the *doing* of Creative Writing might have a function we acknowledge what Karin Knorr-Cetina refers to in her work in an alternative field as 'ad-hoc decisions' and 'unpublished know-how', as well as what Cecil Day-Lewis refers to as 'questioning'. In addition, what Cynthia Ozick refers to as 'breathing inside a blaze of words' and what John Updike refers to as 'turning inklings into thoughts and thoughts into words'. All this has relevance to the undertaking of Creative Writing and how we understand it.

This likewise suggests that to talk of a system by which Creative Writing occurs would not be beyond reasonableness. A system that initiates, encourages, causes or supports functions. Here then, a point of potential controversy! A system of Creative Writing? Surely this goes against a notion of art, as well as challenging the idea of real freedom, true individuality, given that a system must be something that is in some way identifiably organised, identifiably structured. Equally, such a suggestion must represent a reductionist approach to Creative Writing whereby acts and actions can be placed in some kind of conceptual grid, connected as if wired together to create, indeed, the machine or device that the word 'system' seems to point towards.

But, of course, this is not the suggestion at all. Nor is the use of system here that which carries the linguistic baggage of its incorporation in recent physicalist ideals whereby cultural or social phenomenon, alongside technologies, living alongside the living (the former the thing possessed, the latter *the action undertaken*), are presented as if components in tangible environments. The term 'system' is thus better considered in terms of its adjectival form: the *systemic*. This is not to do with the well-known area of systems art[1] where discussions of systems also incorporate the system as medium; rather, the term systemic here refers to concepts, ideas, assumptions, tendencies which work together to bring about Creative Writing.

Creative Writing is systemic also in that the acts and actions of Creative Writing, and the works that are produced, are subject to holistic change as well as general evolution, so that while we might talk about the learning of particular compositional skills or even of singular conceptual or concrete *abilities* the nature of Creative Writing as systemic means that one element interacts with another. Changes, developments or increases in one ability don't occur without some likelihood of associative impact elsewhere. How creative writers respond to this associative condition can additionally show systemic connections.

We can also consider the systemic nature of Creative Writing in terms of choice – in this sense, using the idea of system to refer to both conscious and unconscious choices that can be made by creative writers in Creative Writing. This is similar, if not identical, to the sense in which the term system is frequently used in the field of linguistics. In linguistics the meaning relates to 'competing possibilities among the grammatical or lexical elements of a language, often considered with a set of statements for choosing among the possibities'.[2]

So the systemic entails competing writerly choices and the question of how, and when, and in what form those choices are made, with what results. That is, whether the results are considered successful or unsuccessful by the creative writer and in what ways these choices produce works or contribute to the working. This may also relate to how a creative writer establishes, within the context of their Creative Writing, a paradigm of behaviour and results that equate with their own definitions, and assessments, of utility, achievement, aesthetic worth, progression, communication and, indeed art. Their consideration of the nature of acts and actions then becomes paramount.

2.

Is Creative Writing something that happens to us, or is Creative Writing something that we do? A question posed rhetorically. Yet, it is easy enough to revisit this question with a slightly more investigative thrust, and explore an intriguing phenomenon. Thus: is it possible that when Creative Writing is undertaken the creative writer is in a particular frame of mind, a particular mode of engagement (with the self, those around her or him, with the world) and that this occurs according to a focus on act and action? While works emerge from these activities, might there thus be a fundamental difference between works that emerge in Creative Writing pre-working, working, complementary-working and post-working and 'final' or 'completed' works that are released in some way by the creative writer?

Actions, by philosophic definition, are considered to be 'what we do'. The term is used slightly differently in this book; but just to pursue this more general definition, momentarily: actions, as what we do, involve active doing – in which we cause something to happen, or something to be done. Of course, some things we do would not, by this definition, be considered actions. That is, things that happen to us, where we are passive receptors of activity. Perhaps the most commonly used example of this is sneezing – where something obviously occurs and we obviously are involved in it; but we are not intentionally undertaking it and, in that respect, we most often didn't act as agents of causation, merely as agents of delivery. We can see here obvious associations with the history of how we have viewed creating. As Rob Pope points out:

Only gradually and fitfully did a specifically human sense of agency creep into the meaning of 'create'. But even then human powers of creation tended to be tinged – or tainted – with a divine aura.[3]

And so it also could be said of the association between agent and action in Creative Writing: it can be tinged with suggestions that we do not have clear causal power. The intention, the will, the desire, that brings about numerous acts of Creative Writing involves personal choice. But it also involves neurological activity that is sometimes independent of such choice. This may occur in terms of style or shape, pace or structure, word choice or paragraph placement in Creative Writing, to name just a little of what we might think of as technical skills – though acting on them is not necessarily brought about by our intentional doing. And that's the point.

Again, seemingly we're heading in a direction of either looking toward the divine (and thus abdicating responsibility) or even of suggesting that Creative Writing is something that happens via a version of akrasia (or weakness of will)[4], whereby we undertake Creative Writing because somehow something against good judgement overcomes us! What is more accurately acknowledged is that it is possible for us to not act passively but still without attentional motivation. In other words, to act through an element of automated understanding that is cognitively 'deeper' than conscious intention. Colloquially speaking it is therefore 'unsupervised' by us, and that is thus independent of our agential choice. That does not make it 'not of us'. Nor does it make such action occur without the possibility of self-deception: we may act without attention, informed by a deep neurological mapping, but such action is certainly not epistemologically privileged. However, this does alert to the fact that attention and awareness, while part of the acts and actions of Creative Writing, are not the sole defining elements associated with it. In this sense, we could indeed say that Creative Writing is something that we do and that it is also something that happens to us. We can say that it thus can be learnt, and therefore taught, but we need to acknowledge that some of its elements involve long term neurological developments. Less esoterically, we could point to its works to note that Creative Writing also becomes *physically manifest beyond ourselves,* exemplifying the functions of writing as mnemonic, and as bridging spatial and temporal distance. In doing so, and in doing this at several levels of release of works, within our personal spaces or involving a wider readership or audience, the existence of works of Creative Writing is never neutral in aspect or in result. Lisa Maruca touches on this very well, even though she is not pursuing the same subject, in an article on 18th century textual production, when she writes:

> [...] the medium of print has never been and was not always thought to be a pure or neutral form of communication, but one which always conveys and supports a specific ideological regime [...] a narrative about the provenance of knowledge, a struggle between intellectuals and professional writers on one side, and artisans and workers on the other [...] print transforms from the work of the body to the carrier of the mind. And despite the Romantic Author's rejection of all things commercial, the moral of this story illustrates that the rise of authorship went hand in hand with the creation of the print text as commodity. This idea turns our standard teleology on its head, as it poses the Author as the creator of print, rather than vice-versa. The ideology of authorship deployed for its own benefit an enduring vision of print as fixed, standardized, and invisible. To adopt these notions as an 'essential' aspect of the print medium is to accede to this regime.[5]

'The Author as the creator of print' – it's a statement that has a similar feel to 'Creative Writing is something that we do', and could just as easily be brushed aside as truism. Any yet, as Maruca makes clears, the reverse interpretation is very well known – the notion of print creating author – and has had a considerable influence on how we have viewed the relationship between creative writer and works of Creative Writing. The provenance of knowledge in which knowledge 'was disseminated only through *sweat* and *labour* and *letter* [...] three terms [...] which cannot be separated'[6] [my italics] is not incongruous with the idea of Creative Writing as divinely informed or unfathomably delivered by some weakness of will to resist doing so; nor is it far removed from questions about the role of readers and audiences in making texts. However, such suggestions fail to understand the nature of intentional and unintentional action in Creative Writing, action that is brought about by conscious choice and action that occurs because we have the neurological inclination and information to initiate it occurring. Acts and actions thus manifest in works of Creative Writing and, though the question of in whose provenance these works then reside might be debated, there is little doubt that the works themselves represent the creative writer as maker and that these are manifestations of that fact.

Notes

1. See, for example, Halsall, F. (2008) *Systems of Art: Art, History and Systems Theory*. Oxford: Peter Lang, for a lively exploration of this systems art and associated discussions.
2. Trask, R.L. (1993) *A Dictionary of Grammatical Terms in Linguistics*. London: Routledge, p. 274.
3. Pope, R. (2005) *Creativity: Theory, History, Practice*. London: Routledge, p. 38.
4. Akrasia is defined as 'weakness of will; acting in a way contrary to one's sincerely held moral values', *Collins English Dictionary* (2003) Glasgow: Collins.
5. Maruca, L. (2003) Bodies of type: the work of textual production in English printers' manuals. *Eighteenth-Century Studies* 36(3), Spring 2003, 338.
6. Maruca, L. (2003) Bodies of type: the work of textual production in English printers' manuals. *Eighteenth-Century Studies* 36(3), Spring 2003, 328.

Chapter 12

Personal and Social Activities Relating to Creative Writing are Always Connected?

1.

> The writer [...] does depend on his environment, and it is important to understand just where his own, personal, work begins. It is not in the demonstration of a positive truth: even if he is inspired by such a truth – as Stendhal in his dependence on the Ideologists, Zola on Claude Bernard and Dr Lucas, Surrealism on psychoanalysis – he is not their discoverer.[1]

An impassioned call from its writer, Yvon Belaval, in this article entitled *The Author and Love*, published in *Yale French Studies* in the mid-20th century. The question here is perhaps not where the creative writer's 'own, personal, work begins' but where it ends. In a Bergsonian sense, there might be said to be no division at all between the actions of a social situation and the actions of a personal one. On the other hand, common-sense tells us that social conditions vary with regard to creative writers and Creative Writing, and the conditions pertaining to an individual writer's personal environment, individual circumstance, individual disposition and individual state of mind.

Society can be considered as an entity, in its own right; with its own holistic set of rules, structures and functions. So while Bergson's sense of fluidity of action is productive in differentiating between a sense of time that falsifies in separating one moment, one action, from the next – that is, by treating time as compartmentalised 'bits' – it is not quite as useful in dealing with actions that occur according to individualist or holistic situations; that is, with contrasting what occurs within a personal sphere and what happens within a societal one.

Society, considered as a holistic entity, involves collective agreements of some kind (for example, even the general definition of 'what is a story?' Or 'what is poetry?' can come into this category). Again, commonsense

94

tells us this is the case because without some kind of collective agreement whatever society it might be would not survive; indeed, it would be unlikely to form in the first place. Shared understandings – at least some – exist to make societies. Shared histories – however these might be interpreted by sub-groups within society or by individuals – form the basis of a collective conscious. The existence of a society generates structures that support it, as well as processes and functions and roles that perpetuate and legitimate the society's existence[2]. Societies encourage modes of action, often support some modes over others, and encourage systems of their day-to-day operation that, while encompassing change, encourage societal survival.

This, above, is a version of holistic analysis. Were we to shift toward an emphasis on individualism then, while it would not be denied that societies exist, it would be stressed that society as a whole is not an entity that easily bears a concerted examination, reducing always to the actions of individuals and groups, group and individual interpretations and functions, and this portioning of society is what makes a macro societal analysis neither really possible nor, more importantly, particularly accurate. Neither the holist approach nor the individualist approach would suggest that individuals (or agents [of action], as each of us can be called in the context of this analysis) always act in a way that matches the requirements or rules or structures that society entails. Nor would it be true to say that all agents always act in a way that is good, most productive, or best undertaken, for themselves. Sometimes, that is, individuals act irrationally, without much thought, or against their own best judgement as result, for example, of emotion, feeling, flawed reasoning.

For closer consideration of all this, the title of Belaval's article, *The Author and Love*, serves as a useful mnemonic. Talking of a 'social act' of love carries a number of perhaps positive, perhaps negative, connotations; but, regardless of how a social expression of love might occur, there's little doubt that it is something conceptually different to a 'personal act' of love. And, indeed, Belaval attempts to argue for such a separation with his post-event analysis of the work of creative writers in contrast to that of scientists, suggesting that the work of a scientist is 'impersonal and anonymous'[3] while the work of a creative writer is to surprise a positive truth 'as one surprises a personal secret'.[4] At the same time he declares that 'love remains a social phenomenon because it takes place between people'.[5]

Notions of 'two cultures' aside,[6] the struggle that Belaval is going through relates to how to describe *what is distinct to the personal activities of*

Creative Writing and what is *located in the social activities of Creative Writing*. Mike Sharples, in *How We Write: Writing as Creative Design*, travels over connected territory, though his vista incorporates all kinds of writing not solely Creative Writing. 'An episode of writing starts not in a single idea or intention, but with a set of external and internal constraints,'[7] he says. And: 'at the most general level, the differences between individual writers can be described in terms of where the writer chooses to begin the cycle of engagement and reflection [. . .].'[8] And prior to that: 'how we write is shaped by the world in which we live, with cultural differences affecting not just the language we use but also the assumptions we have about how the written text will be understood and used.'[9]

Sharples is a lively, informed commentator but we are looking here – as his last statement best proves – at the previously noted difference between other forms of writing and Creative Writing, correctly understood in a monistic way as art *and* mode of communication. And yet, Sharples is right to note 'constraints' on writing and make a case for cultural 'shaping' of works and working. These certainly relate to how the personal and societies activities of Creative Writing might connect. But how? How separate are the human activities he mentions in terms of 'cycles of engagement and reflection' and 'the world in which we live'? For the purposes of his design-focused analysis, Sharples is rightly focusing on the micro and macro elements of writing; thus, in his schema, the macro refers to 'an overall structure' of a piece of text, 'that frames the style and content of the text and organizes the expectations of the reader'[10] rather than to the macro entity 'society'.

The problem of discussing the personal and social activities of creative writers, and of Creative Writing, in anything other than a separate fashion appears to be difficult to resolve. On the one hand, it is easy to adopt an individualist perspective and favour a Bergsonian sense of individualist fluidity, as if society does not exist as a holistic entity but only as a collection of individuals. Commonsense tells us that this suggestion has flaws, not least because the structures and functions of society and, indeed, culture don't logically reduce to only the actions of one or other individual, even if individuals retain their individuality within society. On the other hand, a holist perspective merely reduces creative writers to components and pays too little attention to free will and individual disposition. A way to overcome this problem is to look at Creative Writing and creative writers in terms of the *identity* of the activities that are undertaken; and how these activities relate to the identities of creative writers, personally, and socially. In this way, discourse, collective identification, ideologies, symbolisation, social patterns of expectation and sense of self all play a role. Sociologist Karen Cerulo refers to this approach to self and society as a 'synthesis'[11] but it is more likely that considering the personal and social activities relating to Creative Writing as a relational dynamic system gets us to the ways in which Creative Writing as personal endeavour and Creative Writing as societal or cultural activity, occurs.

2.

The more or less connected/disconnected elements of Creative Writing can be grouped under several headings – not for this to suggest that they always exist and operate separately; but, rather, to place them in a neural network, where priorities and hierarchies operate according to historical and cultural context, individual personalities, economic and political circumstance; and where these can be considered either at the point of a singular event (that is, something occurring at a given moment) or in terms of a cycle activity (such as the recurring elements of economic prosperity and downturn, or even of birth and death under which certain individuals or groups may be influential and then, as they reach the end of their lives, others emerge to replace them) or in relation to longer processes of development, change, evolution, which is so protracted as to appear almost fixed. These more or less connected/disconnected elements can include:

(1) individual disposition and personality. The personal traits of a creative writer, while influenced by surroundings, events, and other individuals and groups; this relates to the results and extent of the exchange between individual human *nature* and *nurture*;

(2) cultural and social environments. These might be considered as fixed in time, evolving or cyclical, and the degree to which Creative Writing activities will be connected will depend on the intersection personal trait and cultural or social conditions;

(3) groups and networks. These can include such things as artistic connected associations (those who feel an affinity of aesthetic under-standing with each other or shared beliefs and influences); like-wise ethnic or racial groups, networks defined by shared political ideals or economic aims; those brought together by geography or by nation; groups arising out of adversity; networks established as 'virtual' communities on the WWW or other specific technologies; networks founded on sites of education. The list could go on;

(4) psychological and physiological attitudes to Creative Writing. The individual nature of these limits their social exchange; and yet,

one or other creative writer may relate a material condition with another (creative writers who treat words as concrete or visual art, for example, and whose physiological bond with Creative Writing reflects this) or creative writers who, psychologically, favour public presentation of their work. If these form the basis of action, particularly of post-writing or pre-writing, then connection could happen;

(5)   the role of intermediaries. Publishers or producers, whose intention is to bring works of Creative Writing to a readership or audience, notably as a commercial enterprise. Arts managers in venues or at events whose role is either mostly commercial and/or mostly cultural, privately or publicly funded with the aim of creating event. Educational intermediaries whose focuses are skills-based or cultural, who may be more or less influenced by cultural hegemonies. Who, as the subject of Creative Writing has evolved in universities and colleges, may have an interest in patterns of Creative Writing pre-working, complementary-working and post-working, as well as in completed works;

(6)   personal creative environments. This can include the daily working conditions of the creative writer, their individual relationships, the role of local or private states of existence and how these influence feelings, reasons, emotions and behaviour patterns;

(7)   the speed at which change enters the creative writer's personal world. This can be the product of geography, technology or disposition. It can relate to the degree of interdependence between personal and social worlds that the creative writer requires to survive (for example, change can be disruptive to behaviour or it be integral to maintenance of these patterns);

(8)   the representational or iconic condition that the creative writer's final works occupy. Here the degree of personal and social interactivity – including that connected with pre-works or complementary-works – specifically relates to how the creative writer is seen (or not seen) as representative and how they, and/or intermediaries, manage this representative position.

These are all relatively open suggestions, and no doubt foster even more thought as to where the personal and the social in Creative Writing form nodes of influence. They are not, as could be suggested, synthesised into a singular entity or singular engagement with the world. And, while it is possible to talk of Creative Writing as unified, it is dismissive of one element or another to reduce the personal and social in and around the activities of Creative Writing to a synthesis. A synthesis always involves some dissolution of individual characteristics in preference for the synthesised entity; and this is not the case in Creative Writing. Alternatively, and more productively, we can view the interactions[12] that Creative Writing entails both as internal and external to the creative writer and can see these as happening according to personal as well as historical and cultural patterns, sometimes with clear objectives and intent and sometimes with irresolution.

Notes

1. Belaval, Y. (1953) The author and love. *Yale French Studies* 11, *Eros, Variations on an Old Theme*, 5.
2. I draw here, broadly, on the analysis in C. Lloyd's excellent *Explanation in Social History*. Oxford: Blackwell (1985), but also on K.A. Cerulo's work on culture and cognition.
3. Belaval, Y. (1953) The author and love. *Yale French Studies* 11, *Eros, Variations on an Old Theme*, 5.
4. Belaval, Y. (1953) The author and love. *Yale French Studies* 11, *Eros, Variations on an Old Theme*, 5.
5. Belaval, Y. (1953) The author and love. *Yale French Studies* 11, *Eros, Variations on an Old Theme*.
6. Referring to C.P. Snow's classic argument (1959) that the sciences and the humanities had become increasingly polarised, and communication between them had therefore suffered. Snow, C.P. (1959) *The Two Cultures and the Scientific Revolution.* Cambridge: CUP.
7. Sharples, M. (1999) *How We Write: Writing as Creative Design.* London: Routledge, p. 6.
8. Sharples, M. (1999) *How We Write: Writing as Creative Design.* London: Routledge, p. 8.
9. Sharples, M. (1999) *How We Write: Writing as Creative Design.* London: Routledge, p. 5.
10. Sharples, M. (1999) *How We Write: Writing as Creative Design.* London: Routledge, p. 8.
11. Cerulo, K.A. (1997) Identity construction: New issues, new directions. *Annual Review of Sociology* 23, 400.
12. Milton C. Albrecht offers a supporting argument when he says in an article entitled *Art as an Institution* that 'it is clear that some areas are primarily cultural, others social; some involve psychological aspects, such as the personality of artists or of dealers; many of them are mixed. They involve not one simplified set of relations, but distinct networks of relations and processes within and between areas, which need to be articulated in detail as part of the total operation of the institution. Some of these relations are distinctly harmonious and consistent, but others, for example those between artists and dealers or publishers, imply conflicting aims and purposes. Some aspects,

such as the selection and training of literary artists, are not yet formally organized, as compared with schools of painting and of architecture. These and other aspects need clearer description and analysis before there can be greater certainty about the degree of integration art, in its various forms, has achieved, and how art is sustained as a more or less independent institution with distinct, if not unique, functions in society.' Albrecht, M.C. (1968) Art as an institution. *American Sociological Review*, 33(3), June 1968.

Chapter 13
The Personal and Social Activities of Creative Writing Have Equal Status?

1.

Milton Albrecht, editor of *The Sociology of Art and Literature: A Reader* and former Dean of the University at Buffalo's College of Arts and Sciences, once introduced an article with the statement that he intended to undertake:

> [...] an examination of art as an institution, assuming 'art' as a collective term for a wide variety of aesthetic products including literature, the visual arts, and music, as well as the combined forms of drama and opera. The aspects to be examined will include some general classifications and their implications for the place of art in the social structure, the question of the structure of art as a social institution, the problem of 'basic human need' that art serves, and finally, the question of the universality of art. These aspects represent areas of significance for considering art as an institution, but they also illustrate some major uncertainties and disagreements among sociologists, as well as other social scientists and philosophers.[1]

A dozen years earlier Albrecht had summarised his findings in a related empirical study based on the hypothesis that 'short stories read by large audiences, even though representing distinct reading levels, express essentially the same basic values and ideals of the American family.'[2] He noted:

> [...] our main hypothesis is largely upheld: short stories in wide-circulation magazines, though representing distinct reading levels, reflect cultural norms and values of the American family. In its simplified form, however, this concept of reflection fails to account for significant differences in the frequency with which values occur as main themes.[3]

In both studies, beginning with completed works, Milton Albrecht worked backwards into the text and, finding there recognisable themes and subjects, determined the correlation between completed works of literature and the American society he saw around him. These are laudable pieces of intellectual work, revealing of something about how we use, or situate, finished works of Creative Writing, as well as something – or at least a portion of something – about the place or role of the creative writer as a member of a culture or society. Albrecht's approach is not too far removed from that adopted by Jacqueline Wood, some thirty years later, in her interview of African American playwright and poet Sonia Sanchez, when Wood introduces her interview with:

> Sanchez emerges as an insightful code- breaker, courageously striking a path in her early drama that has contributed to a literary legacy for today's young, successful African American female playwrights. She has interrogated gender boundaries and opened frontiers in language and structure, while producing themes both divisive and threatening to the dynamics of patriarchal black male militant discourse.[4]

Again, an insightful and impressive introduction that situates Sanchez in the social and cultural world in which she works and gives clear voice to how Sanchez can be considered in light of significant themes and subjects that her work encapsulates. It's perhaps not until considering Sanchez's answer to a question about experimentation that we begin to recognise where personal and social activities of Creative Writing regularly involve creative writers plotting a course, and how this course, while not detached from that imagined or interpreted by post-event critics, can involve differing forms of human cartography. Sanchez answers:

> Well, I think what happened is that I just began to look at this thing called playwriting, and because I thought if I'm going to bring something that is different – I mean that's different from just what we were seeing at that time in the American theatre – that I should experiment with not only the language, but experiment with the form.[5]

Sanchez's choice here is almost deferentially offered – 'I *just* began […].' And, beyond the event of Creative Writing, it is also offered with declared speculation – 'well, I *think* what happened is […].' For the creative writer, Sanchez, could it be that the systemic personal elements of creative practice can feel as if they bear little critical weight in an external and post-event intellectual examination? Or could it be simply that 'form' and 'language' are incomplete, or inefficient, linguistic reference points for the Creative Writing that she had undertaken? Could it be, alternatively, that a question about experiment posed after the point of experimenting is devoid of a real example; rather, that it contains the artefactual results of one? Not that Wood poses the question badly; quite the opposite. In fact, she even opens it out by stating 'you seem really open to experimentation' and concluding with 'can you talk about [...]'; thus giving Sanchez plenty of room to move. Still Sanchez searches for ways of revealing action: 'When I did *Sister Sonji* I had nothing to go on. I *just decided*, when I *thought it out* and wrote out what I *wanted to do*; I *kept saying* I don't want a lot of scenery or props on that stage.'[6] Critically, Wood concludes in her Afterword that:

> Sanchez leaves us in a strikingly honest place. As demonstrated in this interview, she redefines what it meant and means to be militant.[7]

No mean task, but perhaps a task of social dimensions defined more by a situating via critical apparatus than one that gives strong voice to Sanchez's compositional acts and actions. Valid knowledge exploration, in either case, of course; and, likewise, due recognition of Sanchez's personal contribution to debate on socially significant issues. But it is interesting to compare Sanchez's searching with Wood's investigating. The two have a relationship, but they are not the same.

When novelist Julian Barnes makes comment on creative writers we see again something of the same air that swirls around the relative status of the personal and the social in Creative Writing:

> Most writers spend most of their time being themselves – that's to say, living through the oscillating self-doubt and mild paranoia, the rival temptations of vanity and self-pity (sometimes voluptuously combined), endemic to the profession. This burden of authorial self is normally quite enough for us.[8]

What, then, is the status of the comments by creative writers on their own acts and actions? Undoubtedly, these comments have a reasonably high status – if the creative writer is recognised within a commercial or cultural commodity market. The personal Creative Writing acts of Sanchez or Barnes, for example, have value not simply because of their Creative Writing itself, but also because both are successful creative writers in the context of the time in which they are writing. In that context, they have status as cultural representatives, and the interest in them as creative writers can be matched by some recognition – albeit the post-event recognition of others – that their subjects or themes have contemporary relevance. Return to a creative writer mentioned earlier – Christine Brooke-Rose – and the status of her acts and actions, framed according to other positions (for example the position: 'experimental novelist') is different again from that of Sanchez or Barnes – though Sanchez has been asked about her 'experimentation' and Barnes's relatively close connections with France might constitute a reason to talk about Barnes and Brooke-Rose, who wrote for most of her life in France, in some connected way. But what sort of 'grouping together' does that entail, and to what purpose? Similarly, when Brooke-Rose announces that 'I shall now try to be a little more specific about what I've been doing'[9] to whom exactly is she speaking? The general reader – whoever that might be? For some, or in some circumstances, the value of her activities could be higher than those of Sanchez or Barnes. But to whom and when?

So far, two aspects are revealed: firstly, that the status of completed works of Creative Writing in representing and transporting cultural norms and values is not diminished over time – even if this status is relative to historical changes in norms and values. And, though lacking Albrecht's empirical evidence, it is safe to say that the results of his study have equal relevance to works of Creative Writing currently given 'wide-circulation' (that is, to 'popular' works) as they did at the time of his study. Secondly, that the status of the personal activities of creative writers, for whatever reason (relating to the period in which they are living), varies to such an extent that even the ability to communicate thoughts about these activities is constrained, or made free, by external as well as internal factors.

2.

Some years before he died Kurt Vonnegut announced 'if I die – and God forbid – I would like to go to heaven to ask somebody in charge up there, "Hey, what was the good news and what was the bad news?"'[10] For creative writers the good news, perhaps, is that both personal and social activities associated with Creative Writing have degrees of status. That is, they have a position relative to other things in the world and it is discernible. This is universally the case anywhere that Creative Writing occurs, and in whatever context. However, there are vast and important variations.

Taking the personal activities first – that is, those occurrences that are of the person (a creative writer) rather than of, or in, a community or group. The acts and actions of Willa Elphinstone (replace this unknown writer with the name of any 'unknown' creative writer) have low status if they are not related to works of commercial or cultural value. This value, set by cultural and societal conditions, impacted upon by political and economic circumstance, and brought about mostly according to human events or the cycles of human history, is not fixed in time or space and does not relate necessarily (or, at least, entirely) to the ability of the creative writer to undertake these acts and actions in an informed or knowledgeable way. What constitutes excellence in works of Creative Writing is not a fixed notion, anymore than what constitutes Creative Writing is fixed.[11] Also, the unknown creative writer can, and does, become part of a wider social environment, and status in this sense can change. Saul Bellow once declared that 'given encouragement, unknown writers, formerly without hope, materialize'.[12] He was commenting on impact of the launch of the magazine collaboration *The Republic of Letters*, founded by Bellow and Keith Botsford. Of course, Bellow is talking here about completed works being submitted to the magazine. 'My friend Keith Botsford and I felt strongly that if the woods were filled with readers gone astray, among those readers there were probably some writers as well'.[13] Likely so, but unless these creative writers released works in some way to the world they will not be known. The acts and actions of Creative Writing occur regardless of their public presentation.

It is not just the commercial or cultural value that impacts on the status of the personal activities of Creative Writing. Creative Writing, like other arts, conveys emotional and attitudinal connections between one human being and another, in a convoy. Even if all works of Creative Writing are not given equal recognition, creative writers whose works are in a public sphere have the positional reference of: pleasure (that is, status conveyed by how much pleasure one or other of their works of Creative Writing offers one or other reader); the stimulation of emotion (as referred to by Tolstoy: 'if successful artists imbue their works with an emotion in such a way as to stimulate the same emotion in their audience,'[14] then status can be conveyed on the actions that produced this bridge); the degree of knowledge that a work is considered to offer the reader or audience (with different forms of knowledge having different value, of course); representational position (again, depending on how the personal activities of a creative writer appear to represent or resemble current cultural or societal values). Of course, it is true to say that the creative writer is engaged in 'a continuous process of self-creation'[15] and these reference points, while reaching between the personal and public, are drawn from the creative writer's consideration and reconsideration of the self.

Returning to Vonnegut, it might be said that 'the bad news' (if that is what it is) is that self-creation and world-creation, or societal-creation, are not often a perfect match. The social activities of Creative Writing, whereby creative writers and their works are involved in (and considered within) society at large have a status substantially impacted upon by history, location and circumstance.[16] Societies, much like individuals, change and adapt; they react to external and internal stimuli (for example, the stimuli of external changes in the natural environment or in the availability of resources; or the internal stimuli of the development of new technologies). If the role and status of the personal activities of Creative Writing – and, in particular, of the personal activities of the individual creative writer – have equality with the social activities of the Creative Writing it is primarily that a confluence is occurring, which will have a length and depth. How long this confluence will continue and how much bearing it will have on the creative writer or on society is finite only at the time we consider it.

Notes

1. Albrecht, M.C. (1968) Art as an institution. *American Sociological Review* 33(3), June 1968, 383.
2. Albrecht, M.C. (1956) Does literature reflect common values? *American Sociological Review* 21(6), December 1956, 722.
3. Albrecht, M.C. (1956) Does literature reflect common values? *American Sociological Review* 21(6), December 1956, 729.
4. Wood, J. (2005) This thing called playwrighting: an interview with Sonia Sanchez on the art of her drama. *African American Review* 39(½), Spring-Summer 2005, 122.
5. Wood, J. (2005) This thing called playwrighting: an interview with Sonia Sanchez on the art of her drama. *African American Review* 39(½), Spring-Summer 2005, 123.
6. Wood, J. (2005) This thing called playwrighting: an interview with Sonia Sanchez on the art of her drama. *African American Review* 39(½), Spring-Summer 2005, 125.
7. Wood, J. (2005) This thing called playwrighting: an interview with Sonia Sanchez on the art of her drama. *African American Review* 39(½), Spring-Summer 2005, 130.
8. Barnes, J. (2003) Literary executions. In M. Arana (ed.) *The Writing Life: Writers on How They Think And Work.* New York: Public Affairs, p. 382
9. Brooke-Rose, C. (2002) *Invisible Author.* Columbus: Ohio State University Press, p. 42.
10. Vonnegut, K. (2007) Here is a lesson in Creative Writing. In K. Vonnegut, D. Simon (ed.) *A Man Without a Country.* New York: Random House, p. 37.
11. Seamus Deane refers to these questions this way: 'There is a strong argument for saying that an artist will be accepted to the degree that s/he "reflects" the condition of a society, although it could be said, with equal force, that a society's condition of itself is reflected in the priority it gives to one writer

over another.' Deane, S. (1990) Society in the artist. *Studies: An Irish Quarterly Review* 79(315), Autumn 1990, 247.

12. Bellow, S. (2001) Hidden within technology's empire, a republic of letters. In J. Darton, *Writers on Writing: Collected Essays from* The New York Times, intro. New York: Holt, p. 22.

13. Bellow, S. (2001) Hidden within technology's empire, a republic of letters. In J. Darton, *Writers on Writing: Collected Essays from* The New York Times, intro. New York: Holt, p. 22.

14. Tolstoy, L. (1995) in A. Neill and A. Ridley (eds) *The Philosophy of Art: Ancient and Modern*. New York: McGraw Hill, p. 511.

15. Kroll, J. (2006) Redrafting the self: the author as a work in progress. In N. Krauth and T. Brady (eds) *Creative Writing: Theory Beyond Practice*. Tenerfife: Post Pressed, p. 207.

16. Richard Carlton, writing on musicians in the 18th century, says 'diverse social organizations such as church or court have differently defined the position of the musician'. The same could be said of the position of the creative writer and of Creative Writing. Carlton, R. (2006) Changes in status and role-play: The musician at the end of the eighteenth century. *International Review of the Aesthetics and Sociology of Music* 37(1), June 2006, 4.

Chapter 14
Communication and Art Hold Equal Status in Society?

1.

It is not possible, not entirely, and not with absolute certainly, to not communicate *somehow* between the personal and social environments. It is possible, of course, to be as remote from contact with other human beings as this planet allows (or, as space travellers have shown, as technology allows). But it is not possible, despite what Jacques Derrida has said about the 'invisible interior'[1] of the 'creative imagination' to remove Creative Writing from some form of communication, whether with the outside world or with a self that is at least partially formed by nurture as well as nature, and a nurture that takes into itself the social and cultural surroundings with which it engages. We are not always in control of this communication – certainly not as children and not entirely as adults either – and whatever personal nature we possess must negotiate between personal desire and need and communal embodiment. Quite simply, considered one of the higher primates we have the inherent characteristic of being social creatures.

Even were we to ignore the commonly touted moral imperative that human beings should engage in 'good communication' with each other, or the development of such vastly used terms as 'communication tecnology', or the vast array of educational situations in which verbal communication, written communication, visual communication, mass communication are considered, we could not ignore the underlying suggestion in all this that the ability to communicate is part of human survival and human life. Whatever else can be said, the difference between a wide consensus about the importance of communication and any consensus about the role of art in human life is that engagement with art is, by its definition as *one* form of human expression, more limited.

Art is, therefore, dependent on its recognition as a significant human activity for reasons commonly associated with such things as the humanising effect of engagement with it; or the emotional roundedness that the arts (sometimes, at a juncture, contrasted with the sciences) can bring about by approaching issues and problems of human existence, or indeed celebrating achievements and wonders; or the elements of pleasure, representation and knowledge that are, more or less, said to exist in any given work of art.

Creative Writing, however, has often been faced with its supposedly dual status as 'writing' that is 'creative'; so assumptions that it carries within it, in a glued-together fashion, the communication practices of an other kind of writing – associated with increasing the range of human memory; creating across distance of time and space; allowing for codification and normalisation; proposing language in concrete form (as opposed to ephemeral spoken language) that can be approached in its own right; and visually physical properties as text – these communication practices are glued together with the ideal of the creative (the preponderance and elevation of the imaginative, the expressive, the original).

As an art form, therefore, Creative Writing should have considerable advantages in conveying its centrality to human existence, with an appeal to universal ideas about communication and with its use of artistic means to convey its communicative strategies. And yet, this is not obviously the case. There are simple reasons for this: Creative Writing as a term to describe the acts and actions of creative writers encompasses a considerable number of practices and, Creative Writing, as a term to define works that emerge from these practices does not produce only one form of art and communication but many.

We have dealt with this variety – certainly in a post-event way – by defining the form and function of completed works according to their material appearances and attributes. So, of course, the novel, a poem, a screenplay, all are defined, and contrasted, by reference to their physical entities. Their purposes, likewise, might be varied, but their communicative and artistic offerings are often treated as functions so that where the personal engagement of the creative writer with acts and actions occurs this is seen as secondary to the functional nature of the completed works within the context of our material definitions. This is further enhanced by commercial and cultural commodification.

So the purpose, function and physical nature of Creative Writing *for the creative writer* might in this schema be referenced barely at all. As the creative writer's personal engagement with Creative Writing involves elements of communication and art in a singular active relationship, rather than two elements at times active or inactive according to material need, then the status of either communication or art is not diminished.

Rather, for the creative writer both hold equal status and both are involved in the monistic activity that is Creative Writing.

However, this is not the same as the status of works of Creative Writing in society because these works are considered to be both a form of communication and one example of a work of art. They compete, thus, between other forms of communication – in terms of utility as well practicability in relation to the time taken for composition, for example, or the plain transference of ideas or instructions – which may have higher general applicability, and they compete against other arts, which may be thought to have greater value due to their uncommonness.

The last point needs a little unpacking. Simple, because Creative Writing most often uses readily identifiable forms in its using of words, even if these words are used in complex or uncommon ways, it is what might be called a 'domesticated' art form. Its links with human communication, more generally, is highly developed – as an aspect of human evolution and therefore as a component of human advancement. Nelson Goodman reminds us of this when he says in his book *Ways of Worldmaking*, that 'we can have words without a world but no world without words or other symbols'.[2]

Words are not alone in their ability to form, to 'make', but the expectation of communication, plain and simple or associated with instruction or information or declaration, is not directly related to the status of written words themselves. Goodman offers some more of this when saying:

> Fiction, then, whether written or painted or acted, applies truly neither to nothing nor to diaphanous possible worlds but, albeit metaphorically, to actual worlds. Somewhat as I have argued elsewhere that the merely possible – so far as admissible at all – lies within the actual, so we might say here again, in a different context, that the so-called possible worlds of fiction lie within actual worlds. Fiction operates in actual worlds in much the same way as nonfiction.[3]

Of course, the difference not noted in Goodman's outline above is that the written carries higher law (that is, rule) status than the painted. While open to interpretation, the written is, aiming to reduce the possibility of misinterpretation and, while involving reification, to nevertheless standardise and prescribe language. Were works of Creative Writing actually made up of the two components, writing and the creative, which of course they are not, it would be the creative that was bringing tension into a medium that was meant to establish and promote clear denotation.

2.

According to Mathias Dewatripont and Jean Tirole, whose field is Political Economy, 'effectiveness of communication [...] hinges on *the alignment of the parties' objectives*.'[4] In the case of Creative Writing, and considering the range of works that emerge from Creative Writing, how can we determine where alignment occurs and where it doesn't occur? We can discern that, given communication is generally seen as a principled and demonstrable activity, and is widely promoted in society, that completed works of Creative Writing that communicate norms or ideals clearly between creative writer and reader or audience would be likely to have high status within society, where as those that are less clearly communicating would not. There's an element of truth in this, historical change notwithstanding, in that where elements of social and cultural hegemony favour particular subjects, forms or attitudes at any one time those completed works that clearly demonstrate their interest in these subjects forms or attitudes are likely to be regarded as having higher commercial or cultural value.

And yet, there are flaws in this suggestion. If the 'parties' objectives', to use Dewatripont's and Tirole's term, are separated by market or social group, or if there are not two parties but three – for example, (1) creative writer, (2) publisher or producer, (3) reader or audience – who is it that is required to be aligned? Certainly an alignment of three in this way changes not only communication but the relative status of the works themselves (that is, offering societal or cultural branding or recognition prior to release to the reader or audience). And what about works of Creative Writing that are not intended for dissemination beyond the personal world of the creative writer? Does it really always, as Dewatripont and Tirole suggest, 'take two to communicate.'[5]

It is unfair to pose this question in relation to these political economists, because their intention is not the same as the one here. However, only one sense of 'communicate' or 'communication' involves interpersonal exchange; the other senses include exchanges of thoughts or information or plans, transference of observations or intentions, travailing of those moments of understanding that appear disparate or disconnected. In this case, *intra*personal exchange may be as significant as *inter*personal, and the alignment there, if it is an alignment of moments of thought or action, may well be the alignment of intention and reason, of perceived meaning and maintained feelings.

Enter then the fact that Creative Writing is an art as well as a mode of communication, each and the same, and intrapersonal importance of a creative writer's self-concept, personality, memory, emotion, personal perception becomes as important as the alignment with a external reader or audience. It's a reminder of Seamus Deane's comment that:

> If we adhere to naive reflection theory, whereby there is a correspondence, perfect or imperfect, between what a writer does and what the material conditions of society are, certain assumptions are silently made [...] All of these assumptions are founded on a theory of representation whereby, politically or artistically, one person or one action can be taken to represent the desires or wishes of a great number of others who literally elect or choose that person or work to stand in place of themselves. Reflection theory is founded on a rhetoric of representation; the synecdoche by which a part stands for the whole is legitimated by the approval of the whole for that part as a true representation of itself.[6]

But, of course, the creative writer, while communicating at points with others, might well be not acting as a part of the societal whole, but as a whole in their own right, a singular, individual whole. And while there is correspondence between personal and social activities of Creative Writing they don't at all times have equal status or maintain equal status in all circumstances. The fact that Creative Writing is an art is at once its distinctiveness and its association with other arts. That it is also a mode of communication is borne by it as not merely because it is writing but because art can, and does communicate. Using tools of communication, symbols and graphic depictions that remind even the creative writer themselves of other non-artistic forms does not diminish its societal status. And yet, it has so often been reduced to its mere material existence, as shorthand for trying to grasp its actual nature, and it has so frequently been disassociated from art forms such as music or fine art, as shorthand for recognising its alignments with day-to-day inscription.

Creative Writing bears in its acts and actions, and in its works, the inheritance of our graphical objectifying of language but, most importantly, it bears in the activities of creative writers the inheritance of our human desire to make art from communication, and communication from art, to create worlds from the world we encounter externally, and internally within ourselves, to make these worlds so that they satisfy ourselves and give life to our association with others.

Notes

1. Derrida, J. (1978) *Writing and Difference*. Chicago: University of Chicago, p. 8.
2. Goodman, N. (1978) *Ways of Worldmaking*. Indianapolis: Hackett, p. 6.

3. Goodman, N. (1978) *Ways of Worldmaking*. Indianapolis: Hackett, p. 104.
4. Dewatripont, M. and Tirole, J. (2005) Modes of communication. *Journal of Political Economy* 113(6), 1219.
5. Dewatripont, M. and Tirole, J. (2005) Modes of communication. *Journal of Political Economy* 113(6), 1218.
6. Deane, S. (1990) Society in the artist. *Studies: An Irish Quarterly Review* 79(315), Autumn 1990, 249.

Conclusion

> *[...] So I choose to read the bird as language and the woman as a practiced writer. She is worried about how the language she dreams in, given to her at birth, is handled, put into service, even withheld from her for certain nefarious purposes. Being a writer she thinks of language partly as a system, partly as a living thing over which one has control, but mostly as agency – as an act with consequences.*[1]

Toni Morrison
Nobel Lecture, 7 December, 1993

Acts and actions have consequences. Indeed. These are not always predictable. Nor are they always immediately obvious. Culturally or societally speaking, how we have considered Creative Writing, over time, has been the result of acts over which creative writers have sometimes had limited control. Not to deflect responsibility, however. We have been complicit. How rarely have creative writers challenged the idea that the works released as final works of Creative Writing articulate the entirety of Creative Writing? How seldom has it been mentioned that these works represent a portion of the acts and actions of Creative Writing, interpreted in a certain way and delivered and presented for certain reasons?

Equally, have we often enough celebrated the acts and actions of Creative Writing in and of themselves? This art, this communication offered as a shared, common language between human beings. Have we yet done enough to articulate its real importance? An art that uses the most ordinary of communicative tools and delivers an artistic vision with the most everyday medium. Rather, have we given more attention not to this fact but to particular artefacts that sometimes emerge from a set of Creative Writing activities, not entirely ignoring those that remain out of the public eye or that form the basis of the actions themselves, but not giving these very much consideration either? If this has been the result of commercial or cultural commodity thinking, historically speaking, then what of the importance of Creative Writing to the individual now, to each human being who has experienced, and does experience, it? Creative Writing, after all, is the most human of activities.

Of course, even if in commerce and society we have not always spoken of Creative Writing in this human way, as individuals creative writers have said so very much about their own belief in the acts and actions of Creative Writing that this must surely draw all to realise just how this 'living thing' makes in the world and offers much to it. The knowledge contained in all this is not only knowledge of the structures and forms seen in the recognised artefacts of Creative Writing, not even is it only the physical manifestations of writerly actions, but it is also that associated with individual human intentions, with feelings, reasons and meanings. Creative Writing involves behaviour patterns and human dispositions, perceptions and memories. It is both working and works, not separated, and not placed in a hierarchy determined by external forces but a continuity derived from the simple equation: to be a creative writer means undertaking Creative Writing. To compartmentalise the artefacts of Creative Writing, one from another, or to devolve actions from artefact, or to impose a timeframe associated with the grasping of time or thought in portions, in lumps, does little to explore Creative Writing.

The tendency to see Creative Writing as an informer of materiality, in which works carry forth the matter of Creative Writing is worthy of further investigation, hopefully in the not too distant future. Why does Creative Writing have to inform anything other than itself – so that while material objects might emerge from it, the range of acts and actions undertaken are as valid a site of knowledge and understanding, of human endeavour and human value as any object which might eventually find physical form? And what then of the *association of event* that forms much of Creative Writing? Indeed, that informs the exchange of Creative Writing working and works between human beings. Similarly worthy of further thought is the notion that Creative Writing involves a privileged kind of hard work that means that the creative writer does not so much complete works as grow so weary, so overburdened by the activity itself, that eventually they abandon a work to 'completeness', to finality, no longer having the energy boosting rush of inspiration to maintain them. Why should this be so? Could it be that we've not yet investigated closely enough the ways in which human beings create works of art, and thus fall eventually into a belief that these activities are just slightly beyond our human abilities and therefore belong, more appropriately, in the realm of the 'divine'?

Posing questions often raises further questions. But there's always the aim of finding answers. The answers to the question in this book should already be clear. **Creative Writing primary involves finished works?** No, Creative Writing primarily involves a great deal more than finished works, but finished works are a part of it. **Acts and actions of Creative Writing can be observed in finished works?** Not really. They have been there, no doubt. But the finished works of Creative Writing, often defined by so much beyond Creative Writing and often found by readers and audiences because things well beyond Creative Writing do not provide the clearest window to Creative Writing. Should they? Could they? Does it matter if they do not? Again, it should be clear that the answer is plainly: not really. **No unfinished works are created by creative writers?** Far from it: unfinished works are the marrow in Creative Writing itself, the essential part. Creative Writing does not begin when it ends. **All works of Creative Writing are disseminated?** Hardly! Whether for commercial, cultural or personal reasons most works of Creative Writing are not disseminated. Most works of Creative Writing circulate in the small realms of a creative writer's domestic space, or they pass through the air of inconsequence where culture or commercial worth dispels them. More works of Creative Writing are not disseminated and, in this, might well lie one clue to the humanness of Creative Writing. **There is always a direct relationship between acts and actions of Creative Writing and disseminated works?** No. How could there *always* be when disseminated works most often come to be disseminated for holistically determined reasons indirectly associated with individual writerly actions? **The activities constituted as Creative Writing can always be grouped under the term 'process'?** Process is not the best term. Certainly it is a term trying to grasp something; but what it misses out is as telling as what it includes. To better incorporate fortuitousness, irrationality and emotionality, as well as planned action and rationality, talking of the activities of Creative Writing is far better.

The human engagement with Creative Writing is considerable and shows no signs of diminishing. And yet, questions arise. **All works of Creative Writing have aesthetic appeal?** No. Nor can they be expected to have such appeal when the works of Creative writing emerge for many reasons, not all of them connected with art. **All works of Creative Writing clearly communicate?** As a mode of communication, Creative Writing comes in many forms and takes many approaches and, given that, they cannot possibly all clearly communicate to all people, at all times, in all circumstances. More important, however, is the realisation that Creative Writing is a particular, individual form of communication. **Intentions in Creative Writing are always met?** Intentions form a part of the network of intended and unintended activities and results that are

Creative Writing. They are not always met, but neither are they inconsequential. **Creative Writing is solely an act or range of acts?** Clearly not: Creative Writing also produces physical evidence, artefacts, works. Quite naturally. **Personal and social activities relating to Creative Writing are always connected?** Not always; nor are they always disconnected. Influences occur because of such things as: individual disposition and personality; cultural and social environments; groups and networks; psychological and physiological attitudes to Creative Writing; the role of intermediaries; personal creative environments; the speed at which change enters the creative writer's personal world; the representational or iconic condition that the creative writer's final works occupy. **The personal and social activities of Creative Writing have equal status?** History and context – reference points that are essential, though perhaps generically over-used. But here they have a specific intention: societal creation and self-creation do not match by definition, even if at points confluence occurs. The status of the personal activities of Creative Writing vary greatly, throughout time and place, culture and individual. Equality is perhaps not to be expected, even if its likelihood can be imagined. And, finally: **Communication and art always hold equal status in society?** Creative Writing bears in its activities our human desire to make art from communication, and communication from art. But communication and art often occupy different statuses within societies and cultures and for individuals and groups. The imperative of human communication, in the interests of societal cohesion, is often very strong. Yet art, the reason for it, and the reason we celebrate it, carries its own human significance, its own strong interpersonal and intrapersonal engagements. Equality, then, may not be the most useful way to approach this relationship; but the relationship itself, between one and the other, is of considerable importance.

Creative Writing is human acts and actions, producing more or less a range of artefacts, some long recognised, some unnoticed, some only beginning to be acknowledged. Creative Writing clearly does not happen simply to create material, commercial or cultural objects; nor does it happen always without producing some kind of artefact or artefacts. How these artefacts are valued is determined greatly by commercial, societal and cultural conditions, but not by this only or solely. Creative writers themselves have systems of value and understanding, based in their activities, their analysis of the site of the event of Creative Writing. Creative Writing investigates, explores, articulates and speculates. It is both communication and art, and it moves fluidly between these things in a monistic, connected way that cannot be distilled into convenient pots, or stopped and taken away for examination as if by beginning with material object under a scalpel will reveal the true living thing. And yet, it can certainly be considered, and it should be considered, in motion, in practice. Creative Writing is, after all, one of our most enduring and most significant human activities.

Notes

1. Morrison, T. (2008) Nobel lecture. In *What Moves at the Margins*. Jackson: University of Mississippi, p. 199.

Bibliography

Adorno, T. (1994) *Minima Moralia*. London: Verso.

Albrecht, M.C. (1956) Does literature reflect common values? *American Sociological Review* 21(6), December 1956.

Albrecht, M.C. (1968) Art as an institution. *American Sociological Review* 33(3), June 1968.

Allott, M. (1973) *Novelists on the Novel*. London: Routledge.

Arana, M. (ed.) (2003) *The Writing Life: Writers on How They Think and Work*. New York: Public Affairs.

Atwood, M. (2002) *Negotiating with the Dead: A Writer on Writing*. Cambridge: Cambridge University Press.

Atwood, M. (2005) *Writing with Intent: Essays, Reviews, Personal Prose, 1983–2005*. New York: Carroll & Graf.

Auster, P. (1998) *The Art of Hunger*. London: Faber.

Barth, J. (1980) *Letters: a Novel*. London: Secker and Warburg.

Barth, J. (1995) *Further Fridays: Essays, Lectures and Other Nonfiction, 1984–1994*. Boston: Little Brown.

Barthelme, D. (1998) K. Herzinger (ed.) *The Teachings of Donald B*. New York: Vintage.

Belaval, Y. (1953) The author and love. *Yale French Studies* 11, *Eros, Variations on an Old Theme*.

Berg, A.S. (1997) *Max Perkins: Editor of Genius*. New York: Riverhead.

Bergson, H. (1910) F.L. Pogson (trans.) *Time and Free Will: An Essay on the Immediate Data of Consciousness*. London: George Allen and Unwin.

Bergson, H. (1998) *Creative Evolution*. New York: Dover. First published in English in 1911.

Bergson, H. (1911) *Matter and Memory*. (N.M. Paul and W. Scott Palmer, trans.) London: George Allen and Unwin.

Blotner, J. (ed.) (1977), *Selected Letters of William Faulkner*. New York: Random House.

Bohm, D. (1998) L. Nichol (ed.) *On Creativity*. London: Routledge.

Boylan, C. (1993) *The Agony and the Ego: the Art and Strategy of Fiction Writing Explored*. Penguin: London.

Brewer, J. (1997) *The Pleasures of the Imagination: English Culture in the Eighteen Century*. London: Harper-Collins.

Brooke-Rose, C. (2002) *Invisible Author: Last Essays*. Columbus: Ohio University Press.

Brooke-Rose, C. (2006) *Life, End Of*. Manchester: Carcanet.

Brown, S.J. (1922) A Catholic library for Dublin. *Studies: An Irish Quarterly Review* 11(42), June 1922.

Burke, S. (ed.) (1995) *Authorship from Plato to the Postmodern: a Reader.* Edinburgh: Edinburgh University Press.

Carey, J. (2005) *What Good Are the Arts?* London: Faber.

Carter, R. (1993) *Introducing Applied Linguistics.* London: Penguin.

Cerulo, K.A. (1997) Identity construction: New issues, new directions. *Annual Review of Sociology* 23, 400.

Cheever, J. (1991) *The Journals of John Cheever.* New York: Knopf.

Chekhov, A. (1988) L. Hellman (ed.) *The Selected Letters of Anton Chekhov.* London: Picador.

Claydon, C. (1989) *Women and Writing in South Africa: A Critical Anthology.* Marshalltown: Heinemann.

Cole, T. (1988) *Playwrights on Playwriting.* New York: Hill and Wang.

Conroy, F. (1999) *The Eleventh Draft: Craft and Writing Life form the Iowa Writers Workshop.* New York: Harper Collins.

Cooper, D. (ed.) (1995) *A Companion to Aesthetics.* Oxford: Blackwell.

Cosgrove, J. and Morgan, M. (2000) The leisure activities of fifth grade pupils and their relationships to pupils' reading achievements. *The Irish Journal of Education/Iris Eireannach an Oideachais* 31.

Coulmas, F. (1999) *The Blackwell Encyclopedia of Writing Systems.* Oxford: Blackwell.

Darnton, J. (2001) *Writers on Writing: Collected Essays from The New York Times.* New York: Holt.

Davies, R. (1990) *A Voice from the Attic: Essays on the Art of Reading.* London: Penguin.

Dawson, P. (2005) *Creative Writing and the New Humanities.* Oxford: Routledge.

Day-Lewis, C. (1957) *The Poet's Way of Knowledge.* Cambridge: Cambridge University Press.

Deane, S. (1990) Society in the Artist. *Studies: An Irish Quarterly Review* 79(315), Autumn 1990.

Delbanco, A. (1999) The Decline and Fall of Literature. *The New York Review of Books* 46(17), 4 November 1999.

Derrida, J. (1978) *Writing and Difference.* Chicago: University of Chicago.

Dewatripont, M. and Tirole, J. (2005) Modes of communication. *Journal of Political Economy* 113(6).

Dinesen, I. (1956) Interviewed by E. Walker. *The Paris Review* 14, Autumn 1956.

Eco, U. (1995) *Six Walks in Fictional Woods.* Cambridge (MA): Harvard University Press.

Edel, L. and Powers, L.H. (eds) (1988) *The Complete Notebooks of Henry James.* New York: OUP.

Egri, L. (1960) *The Art of Dramatic Writing.* New York: Simon and Schuster.

Evans, M. (ed.) (1985) *Black Women Writers: Arguments and Interviews.* London: Pluto.

Fitzgerald, F.S. (1987) *Afternoon of an Author: A Selection of Uncollected Stories and Essays.* New York: Scribner.

Fitzgerald, S. (ed.) (1979) *The Habit of Being: The Letters of Flannery O'Connor.* New York: Vintage.

Friedman, D. (2007) *The Writer's Brush: Paintings, Drawings and Sculpture by Writers.* Minneapolis: Mid-List.

Fugard, A. (1983) M. Benson (ed.) *Notebooks of Athol Fugard: 1960–1977*. London: Faber.

Gardner, H. (1993) *Creating Minds*. New York: Basic.

Gardner, J. (1991) *The Art of Fiction: Notes on Craft for Young Writers*. New York: Vintage.

Gass, W. (1978) *The World Within the Word*. New York: Knopf.

Gass, W. (1996) *Finding a Form*. Ithaca: Cornell.

Ghosh, R.K. (1987) Artistic communication and symbol: some philosophical reflections. *British Journal of Aesthetics* 27(4), Autumn 1987.

Ginsburg, A. (1990) *Indian Journals: Notebooks, Diaries, Blank Pages, Writings*. London: Penguin.

Goff, M. (ed.) (1989) *Prize Writing*, London: Sceptre.

Golding, William, *The Hot Gates and other Occasional Pieces*, New York: Pocket, 1967.

Goodman, N. (1978) *Ways of Worldmaking*. Indianapolis: Hackett.

Graham, G. (1997) *Philosophy and the Arts: An Introduction to Aesthetics*. London: Routledge.

Grew, E.M. (1946) The Creative Faculty. *Music and Letters* 27(2), April 1946.

Grass, G. (1985) *On Writing and Politics: 1967–1983*. San Diego: Harcourt.

Grayson, J. (2001) *Vladimir Nabokov*. Woodstock: Overlook.

Hamburger, M. (1996) *The Truth of Poetry*. London: Anvil.

Hargie, O.D.W. (1997) *The Handbook of Communication Skills*, London: Routledge.

Harper, G. & Kroll, J. (eds) (2008) *Creative Writing Studies: Practice, Research and Pedagogy*. Clevedon: Multilingual Matters.

Harper, G. (2008) *The Creative Writing Guidebook*. London: Continuum.

Harper, G. *New Writing: the International Journal for the Practice and Theory of Creative Writing*. Abingdon: Routledge.

Halsall, F. (2008) *Systems of Art: Art, History and Systems Theory*. Oxford: Peter Lang.

Henry, D. (2000) *Breaking Into Print: Early Stories and Insights into Getting Published*. Boston: Beacon.

Hesse, H. (1973) *Autobiographical Writings*. London: Picador.

Hoffman, M.J. and Murphy, P.D. (1996) *Essentials of a Theory of Fiction*. London: Leicester University Press.

Hotson, L. (1942) Literary serendipity. *ELH* 9(2), June 1942.

Hunter, J.P. (1990) *Before Novels: The Cultural Contexts of Eighteenth Century Fiction*. New York: Norton.

Hughes, T. (2008) *Poetry in the Making: a Handbook for Writing and Teaching*. London: Faber. First published 1968.

Jaszi, P. and Woodmansee, M. (eds) (1994) *The Construction of Authorship: Textual Appropriation in Law and Literature*. Durham (NC): Duke University Press.

Johns, A. (1998) *The Nature of the Book: Print and Knowledge in the Making*. Chicago: University of Chicago Press.

Kaufman, S.B. and Kaufman, J.C. (2009) *The Psychology of Creative Writing*. New York: Cambridge University Press.

Kauvar, E.M. (1996) *A Cynthia Ozick Reader*. Bloomington: Indiana University Press.

Kettle, A. (1962) *An Introduction to the English Novel, Volume One: To George Eliot*. London: Arrow.

Knorr-Cetina, K. (1981) *The Manufacture of Knowledge: An Essay on the Constructivist and Contextual Nature of Science*. Oxford: Pergamon.

Knowles, R. (1996) *Gulliver's Travels: The Politics of Satire*. New York: Twayne.

Krauth, N. and Brady, T. (eds) (2006) *Creative Writing: Theory Beyond Practice*. Tenerfife: Post Pressed.

Levi, P. (1989) *The Mirror Maker: Stories and Essays*. New York: Schocken.

Lloyd, C. (1986) *Explanation in Social History*. Oxford: Blackwell.

Macoby, E.E. (1951) Television: its impact on school children. *The Public Opinion Quarterly* 15(3), Autumn 1951.

Manguel, A. (1996) *A History of Reading*. London: Harper Collins.

Majumdar, R. and McLaurin, A. (eds), *Virginia Woolf*, London: Routledge, 1997.

Marquez, G.G. (2004) *Living to Tell the Tale*. New York: Vintage.

Maruca, L. (2003) Bodies of type: the work of textual production in English printers' manuals. *Eighteenth-Century Studies* 36(3), Spring 2003.

Marr, D. (2008) Patrick White: the White Chapter. *The Monthly* 33, May 2008, 28–42

Marr, D. (1992) *Patrick White: A Life*. Sydney: Vintage.

Marr, D. (1996) *Patrick White Letters*. Chicago: University of Chicago.

McGurl, M. (2009) *The Program Era: Postwar Fiction and the Rise of Creative Writing*. Cambridge, MA: Harvard University Press.

McQuail, D. (1994) *Mass Communication Theory: An Introduction*. London: Sage.

Mehring, M. (1990) *The Screenplay: A Blend of Film Form and Content*. Boston: Focal.

Moore, M. (1961) Interviewed by Donald Hall. *The Paris Review* 26, Summer-Fall 1961.

Morris, B. (1940) Intention and fulfilment in art. *Philosophy and Phenomenological Research* 1(2), December 1940.

Morrison, T. (2008) In C.C. Denard (ed.) *What Moves at the Margin: Selected Nonfiction*. Jackson: University of Mississippi.

Motion, A. (1994) *Philip Larkin: A Writer's Life*. London: Faber.

Myers, D.G. (1996) *The Elephants Teach: Creative Writing Since 1880*. New Jersey: Prentice Hall.

Naipaul, V.S. (2000) *Reading and Writing: A Personal Account*. New York: New York Review of Books.

Nabokov, V. (1974) *Strong Opinions*. London: Weidenfeld and Nicolson.

Neill, A. and Ridley, A. (eds) (1995) *The Philosophy of Art: Ancient and Modern*. New York: McGraw Hill.

Nicholson, V. (2003) *Among the Bohemians: Experiments in Living, 1900–1939*. London: Penguin.

Nin, A. (1986) *The Novel of the Future*. Athens: Ohio University Press.

Oates, J.C. (2005) *Uncensored: Views and (Re)views*. New York: Harper.

O'Brien, E. (2005) The anxiety of influence: Heaney and Yeats and the place of writing. *Nordic Irish Studies* 4.

O'Hanlon, M. (1992) Unstable images and second skins: artefacts, exegesis and assessments in the New Guinea Highlands. *Man*, New Series 27(3), Sept. 1992.

Oldfield, S. (2005) *Afterwords: Letters on the Death of Virginia Woolf*. Edinburgh: Edinburgh University Press.

Ozick, C. (2000) *Quarrel and Quandary*. New York: Knopf.

Ozick, C. (2008) *Dictation: A Quartet*. Boston: Houghton Mifflin Harcourt.

Phillips, L. (ed.) (1988) *F. Scott Fitzgerald on Writing*. New York: Scribner.

Phillips, L. (ed.) (2004) *Ernest Hemingway on Writing*, New York: Scribner.

Pinsky, R. (2005) *Democracy, Culture and the Voice of Poetry*. New Jersey: Princeton University Press.

Pope, R. (2005) *Creativity: Theory, History, Practice*. London: Routledge.

Prince, G. (1988) *Dictionary of Narratology*. Aldershot: Scolar.

Pritchett, V.S. (1974) *Midnight Oil*. London: Penguin.

Proust, M. (1998) *Selected Letters: 1880–1903*. Chicago: University of Chicago Press.

Quiller-Couch, A. (1946) *On the Art of Writing*. Cambridge: Guild, first published 1916.

Regge, T. (1989) *Primo Levi: Conversations*. London: Tauris.

Reiser, O.L. (1924) A monism of creative behaviour. *The Journal of Philosophy* 21(18), 28 August 1924.

Rose, M. (1994) *Authors and Owners: the Invention of Copyright*. Cambridge (MA): Harvard University Press.

Sartre, J.P. (1964) *The Words*. New York: Brazillier.

Schwarz, R.B. (ed.) (2000) *For the Love of Books: 115 Celebrated Writers on the Books they Most Love*. New York: Berkeley.

Sharples, M. (1999) *How We Write: Writing as Creative Design*. London: Routledge.

Snow, C.P. (1959) *The Two Cultures and the Scientific Revolution*. Cambridge: CUP.

Spender, S. (1958) *Great Writings of Goethe*. New York: New American.

Staley, T.F. (2009) Director of the Ransom Centre at The University of Texas at Austin, 'Director's Note', http://www.hrc.utexas.edu/about/director/. Accessed: 14.8.09.

Sullivan, C. and Harper, G. (eds) (2009) *Authors at Work: The Creative Environment*. Cambridge: Brewer.

Thomas, D. (1987) P. Ferris (ed.) *Dylan Thomas: The Collected Letters*. London: Paladin.

Thwaite, A. (1992) *Selected Letters of Philip Larkin: 1940–1985*. London: Faber.

Trask, R.L. (1993) *A Dictionary of Grammatical Terms in Linguistics*. London: Routledge.

Turnovsky, G. (2003) The Enlightenment literary market: Rousseau, authorship, and the book trade. *Eighteenth-Century Studies* 36(3), Spring 2003.

Updike, J. (1968) Interviewed by C.T. Samuels. *The Paris Review* (45), Winter 1968.

Vargas Llosa, M. (1996) *Making Waves: Essays*. New York: Farrar, Straus and Giroux.

Vargas Llosa, M. (1991) *A Writer's Reality*. London: Faber.

Vonnegut, K. (2005) *A Man Without a Country*. New York: Random House.

Watson, H. (2000) Review: Lies and Times: the changing genre of biography. *Reviews in American History* 28(1), March 2000.

Welty, E. (1972) Interviewed by L. Kuehl. *The Paris Review* 55, Fall 1972.

White, E. (2004) *Arts and Letters*. San Francisco: Cleis.

Wood, J. (2005) This thing called playwrighting: an interview with Sonia Sanchez on the art of her drama. *African American Review* 39(½), Spring-Summer 2005.

Woolf, V. (1978) *Between the Acts*. London: Grafton. First published 1941.

Woolf, V. (1981) A. Oliver Bell (ed.) *The Diary of Virginia Woolf: Vol. 2 1920–1924*. London: Penguin.

Yevtushenko, Y. (1963) *A Precious Autobiography*. London: Collins & Harvill.

Index